GROUNDING

FOR THE

METAPHYSICS OF MORALS

Immanuel Kant

GROUNDING for the METAPHYSICS OF MORALS

with

On a Supposed Right to Lie Because of Philanthropic Concerns

third edition

Translated by
James W. Ellington

HACKETT PUBLISHING COMPANY, INC.
Indianapolis/Cambridge

Immanuel Kant: 1724–1804

Grounding for the Metaphysics of Morals was first published in 1785.

Second edition copyright © 1981
    by Hackett Publishing Company, Inc.

Third edition with new material copyright © 1993
    by Hackett Publishing Company, Inc.

Cover design by Listenberger Design Associates
Interior design by James N. Rogers
Printed in the United States of America

Third edition
10 09 08 07 06   8 9 10 11 12

For further information, please address
    Hackett Publishing Company, Inc.
    Box 44937, Indianapolis, Indiana 46244-0937

    www.hackettpublishing.com

Library of Congress Cataloging-in-Publication Data

Kant, Immanuel, 1724–1804.
    [Grundlegung zur Metaphysik der Sitten. English]
    Grounding for the metaphysics of morals: with, On a supposed
right to lie because of philanthropic concerns/Immanuel Kant:
translated by James W. Ellington—3rd ed.
            p.   cm.
    Translation of: Grundlegung zur Metaphysik der Sitten: and of:
Über ein vermeintes Recht aus Menschenliebe zu lügen.
    Includes bibliographical references and index.
    ISBN 0-87220-167-8: ISBN 0-87220-166-X (pbk.)
    1. Ethics.   2. Truthfulness and falsehood.   I. Ellington, James
W. (James Wesley), 1927–   .   II. Kant, Immanuel, 1724–1804.   Über
ein vermeintes Recht aus Menschenliebe zu lügen.   English.   1992.
III. Title.   IV. Title: On a supposed right to lie because of
philanthropic concerns.
B2766.E6E44   1992
170—dc20   92-25359
                                                            CIP

ISBN-13: 978-0-87220-167-5 (cloth)
ISBN-13: 978-0-87220-166-8 (pbk.)

CONTENTS

Foreword   iv

Introduction   v

Selected Bibliography   xiv

GROUNDING FOR THE METAPHYSICS OF MORALS

PREFACE   1

FIRST SECTION
    Transition from the Ordinary Rational Knowledge of Morality   7
    to the Philosophical

SECOND SECTION
    Transition from Popular Moral Philosophy to a Metaphysics of Morals   19

THIRD SECTION
    Transition from a Metaphysics of Morals to a Critique of   49
    Pure Practical Reason

SUPPLEMENT
    On a Supposed Right to Lie because of Philanthropic Concerns   63

German-English List of Terms   69

Index   73

FOREWORD

For the present translation of Kant's *Grounding* I have used Karl Vorländer's German text (Leipzig, 1906) as it appears in Vol. III of the Philosophische Bibliothek edition of Kant's works, and Paul Menzer's text as it appears in Vol. IV of the Königlich Preußische Akademie der Wissenschaften edition of Kant's works. Kant's essay entitled "On a Supposed Right to Lie because of Philanthropic Concerns," which appears as a supplement after the *Grounding*, is to be found in Vol. VIII, pp. 425–30 of the Academy edition. Page numbers of the latter edition, the standard reference for Kant's works, appear in the present translation as marginal numbers. All material interpolated by me in text or notes has been bracketed.

University of Connecticut,   JAMES W. ELLINGTON
Storrs

INTRODUCTION

Kant's moral philosophy is contained in three works: *Grounding for the Metaphysics of Morals* (1785), *Critique of Practical Reason* (1788), and *Metaphysics of Morals* (1797). Some people might want to include *Anthropology from a Pragmatic Point of View* (1798), especially Book III of Part I, where the appetitive power is considered, in order to have something of the empirical basis for morality; some might want to include *Religion within the Bounds of Reason Alone* (1793) in order to have an elaboration of the function of the idea of God in Kant's moral system —an idea that is first introduced in Book II of the *Critique of Practical Reason* ("Dialectic of Pure Practical Reason"). However, in this introduction only the first three works are considered in any detail.

Toward the end of the Preface to the *Grounding* Kant says that the intention of this work is to seek out and establish the supreme principle of morality. This principle is nothing more nor less than the famous categorical imperative: Always act in such a way that you can also will that the maxim of your action should become a universal law. Kant claims that this is the one supreme principle for the whole field of morals, including the philosophy of law (politics) as well as the moral requirements of duties to oneself to maintain one's personal integrity and of duties to others in one's association with them (ethics). For those familiar with Kant's system of theoretic philosophy there is an obvious analogy between the function of the categorical imperative in morals and the function of the transcendental unity of apperception in speculative thought when Kant claims in the *Critique of Pure Reason* (B134 note) that the synthetic unity of apperception is the highest point to which the whole employment of the understanding must be ascribed, even the whole of general logic, and conformable with logic, even the whole of transcendental philosophy. Both principles function as highest synoptic focalpoints to which one is led by all lesser principles and from which one descends to all subsidiary principles. The roles played by these two principles in Kant's philosophy are not unlike those played by the Chief Good in Plato's philosophy and the Prime Mover in Aristotle's philosophy.

The *Grounding* and the *Critique of Practical Reason* both deal with the meta-ethical treatment of the foundations and method of the moral doctrine (or normative ethics) contained in the *Metaphysics of Morals*. The *Grounding* presents moral philosophy as falling under the province of a single supreme principle of pure reason (rather than empirical reason); the *Critique of Practical Reason* investigates the grounds for justifying such a supreme a priori principle (the categorical imperative) as being the fundamental principle of the autonomy of reason in action. As such both works are biased in the direction of high-level abstractions. The *Metaphysics of Morals*, on the other hand, treats of the varied problems of moral judgment and of choice in concrete situations. Moral philosophy is a complex subject, and Kant treats it systematically in these various treatises dealing with one topic at a time.

Kant never claims that he discovered the categorical imperative. In fact he says in the *Critique of Practical Reason* (Ak. 8 note) that it would be outright silly of anyone to claim that he had discovered the moral law as something really new, as if the world up to then had been ignorant of what constitutes moral duty or else had been quite wrong about such duty. This supreme principle is, rather, ordinarily presumed in all moral judgments; it is a working criterion supposedly employed by any rational agent as a guide for making his own choices and judgments but without his being necessarily able to formulate it and make it explicit. If there is a consistent standard according to which everyday actions are judged as being moral or not, then the precise formulation of such a standard would be practically helpful and theoretically enlightening. It is here that Kant claims he has made a worthwhile contribution. He formulates the categorical imperative in some five different ways in the Second Section of the *Grounding*. Each formula is expressed in quite different terms; but when they are properly understood, they can be seen to amount to the same thing. Consequently, Kant has given the world five different formulations of one supreme moral law—not five different moral laws (as some commentators have claimed).

The idea running through all of these formulations is that of autonomy: the moral law is imposed by reason itself and is not imposed externally (heteronomously) as, for example, would be the case if all actions were directed to the attainment of happiness conceived as a state of the subject in which he had no unsatisfied desires but had complete well-being and contentment, or as would be the case if all actions were commanded by the will of God. These various formulations culminate in that of the so-called kingdom of ends. This is the ideal of a moral community in which each member would act in such a way that if all other members acted in this way, then a community of free and equal members would result in which each member would, as he realizes his own purposes, also further the aims of his fellow members. In such a community each member freely disciplines himself under the very same rules that would be prescribed by him for others; the result would be that each member would act as a law unto himself (and hence autonomously) but yet would cooperate harmoniously with every other member.

Such an ideal kingdom of ends has law as its formal ordering principle. Now a law must apply universally and permit no exceptions within its domain. If something is right for me to do, then it must be so for everybody else. In formal terms, the first formulation in the *Grounding* of the categorical imperative states that one should act only on that maxim that can at the same time be willed to become a universal law. A maxim is nothing but a rule that is followed in any deliberately intentional act. To get to Paris, take an Air France flight. In this example there is an aim, the means for attaining it, and the relevant circumstances could be elaborated; in any maxim the aim, means, and circumstances can always be identified. The maxim of an immoral act cannot be willed to become a universal law. When you tell a lie, you do not will that everybody else lie also. For if you did so will, then nobody would believe your lie; and your lying would never work to get you what you want. When you lie, you will that everybody else tell the truth and believe that what you are saying is true, for this is the only way your lie will work. In lying you simply take exception to the law that says everyone should tell the truth.

Clearly from what Kant says in the *Grounding* at Ak. 436, the kingdom of ends has not only a form (the legality examined in the preceding paragraph) but also a matter—its free and equal members and the aims, or purposes, they pursue. To say that they are equally free means that any one of them has not the right either by coercion or deception to subject any of the others to his own private interests. Consequently, another (and oft-quoted) formulation of the moral law states that one should always act in such a way that humanity either in oneself or in others is always treated as an end in itself and never merely as a means. If a person is treated as a mere means, then he is treated as nothing more than a thing without purposes of his own rather than as a self-determining rational agent.

Now despite terminological differences, the formula of the end in itself considered in the preceding paragraph is actually equivalent to the previous formula of universal law. According to the formula of universal law, any violation of the formula of the end in itself must be wrong, i.e., when someone is treated as a mere means, his purposes are regarded as not counting; when the maxim of such treatment is universalized, the agent of such treatment must be willing to be so treated in turn. But here is a contradiction, for no one wants his purposes to count for nothing. Conversely, any violation of the formula of universal law always involves making oneself an exception to the rules (as when one lies). By doing so, he makes the aims of others mere means to his own selfish aims—he exploits others thereby, and the formula of the end in itself forbids such exploitation. Consequently, according to the formula of the end in itself, any violation of the formula of universal law must be wrong. The two formulations mutually imply each other and must therefore be equivalent.

As Kant points out at Ak. 436, when the *unity* of the will's form (universality) is combined with the *plurality* of its matter (will's ends), then there arises a *totality* of the will's system of ends—i.e., a kingdom of ends. The preceding exposition started with the formula of the kingdom of ends and from this formulation distinguished the formula of universal law and the formula of the end in itself. There is still another formulation that derives from the kingdom of ends, viz., the formula of autonomy. The members of this kingdom are not only subject to the rule of law but are also co-authors, or legislators, of the law because of the universalizable maxims according to which they act; thereby is the system a community. Anyone who steps outside this community and imposes law upon the other members without subjecting himself to the law is not treating those members as ends in themselves (i.e., the formula of the end in itself is violated), nor is he regarding his maxims as universal laws (i.e., the formula of universal law is violated). He might employ a system of rewards and punishments to make the members always obey his laws, but they would not do so autonomously. Much the same holds in the case of a religious ethics which conceives of God as a legislator issuing arbitrary commands with threats of damnation unless those commands are obeyed. The formula of autonomy states that one should always act in such a way that his will can at the same time regard itself as legislating in its maxims universal laws. This formula of autonomy is the one that most clearly indicates that a moral imperative must be categorical rather than hypothetical. An imperative is first of all a directive to act in a certain way—it is not a statement of fact. Furthermore, if the imperative is categorical, then the action commanded by it should be done because that action is the right thing to do and not because of some pay-off or advantage offered by the action. A will that obeys a law for an ulterior motive is acting on a hypothetical imperative. A rule that is formally legal (does not violate the formula of universal law) and also just (does not violate the formula of the end in itself) may be put into effect through rewards and punishments. Whoever obeys such a legal and just rule to gain the reward or avoid some penalty, does so for an ulterior motive—his action accords with duty but is not done from duty. He has followed a hypothetical imperative but not a categorical one. For a rule that is both legal and just to be a moral law means that the rule must also be autonomous and in no way dependent upon any ulterior motive; only then is the rule a categorical imperative rather than a hypothetical one.

At Ak. 440 Kant sums up his progress in the first two sections of the *Grounding* by saying that the principle of autonomy is the sole principle of morals and that this has been shown by merely analyzing the concepts of morality. In the process of this analysis the principle of morals is found to be necessarily a categorical imperative, which commands nothing but this very autonomy. Hereby he fulfills the suggestion made at the end of the Preface that the best method will be to proceed analytically from ordinary moral knowledge to a determination of the supreme principle of morality. The working criterion that is reflected in ordinary moral judgments (helping others in distress is good, telling lies is bad, etc.) has been made explicit (though not discovered since that criterion is implicit in every morally good act that was ever done), and that criterion has been given various alternative formulations that reflect the different aspects of that criterion.

But even though the supreme principle of morality has thus far in the *Grounding* been investigated and established, what about that principle itself? How is the principle of autonomy to be justified? It must be justified, or else all the subordinate principles which depend on it (such as the categorical imperative and the principles of jurisprudence and of ethics) will be questionable. The Third Section of the *Grounding* prepares the way, but the *Critique of Practical Reason* has the job of justifying the principle of autonomy. Since this introduction is concerned primarily with the *Grounding*, I shall indicate very briefly what Kant says about the problems of why one should be moral.

Why should one be good unless he thereby attains happiness in this life or else the promise of such in the after-life? As we have already seen, the categorical imperative commands us to be good irrespective of any pay-off. Here we have, of course, the age-old conflict between duty and self-interest. The duty part says there must be a categorical imperative, while the self-interest part says that there are only hypothetical imperatives (do such and such if you want to gain this or that). The conflict involved here concerns mainly a question regarding the possibility of doing whatever is done because of a special kind of incentive, even if other kinds of incentives are present. What sorts of incentives qualify as moral? Can purely rational considerations be sufficient to determine the will to action, not only by providing a rule for distinguishing right from wrong if one wanted to act on that rule, but also by supplying an incentive that is sufficient for performing the action? Purely rational considerations are independent of experience, i.e., are a priori rather than empirical. Practical *action* differs from unintentional or automatic *motion* in that action is rational inasmuch as it is always guided by a conception of what is being done. This conception can always be formulated as a rule or maxim that can logically be nothing but categorical or hypothetical. If the maxim is hypothetical, the action is empirically determined; if categorical, then the action is purely (a priori) determined. The possibility of acting on a categorical imperative means the same thing as the possibility of not being determined to act because of some empirical condition, e.g., someone tells the truth even when telling a lie might promote his personal happiness and comfort. Moral concepts require one to act *from* respect for the idea of conformity to law (incentive) *in accordance with* the capacity of one's maxim to be a universal law (rule) and *for the sake of* (end) a self-regulating community of free members (the kingdom of ends). Not one of these ideas (incentive, rule, end) can be adequately exemplified in experience, and they must therefore all be a priori conceptions.

Insofar as the categorical imperative provides criteria for determining what should be done by pointing out an end, a rule and an incentive, it is a practical principle. But there are certain limitations when one uses this principle to decide about moral character. Any overt action that is contrary to lawfulness (lying, cheating, stealing) is unjust; it is also morally wrong because it could not have been done for any morally acceptable reason. Any action that is unjust and morally wrong is thereby blameworthy. But what about the use of this principle to determine merit? An action may be just (rule) and legal (end) but yet be morally indeterminate (incentive). Does the man who pays his taxes do so because it is the right thing to do or because he wants to avoid the penalties imposed on delinquents; we cannot tell and neither can he really—moral merit can only be known to God, the searcher of hearts.

So, on the one hand, the validity of the categorical imperative implies that there may be causes for action that are independent of empirical influences—i.e., one can act on a priori grounds alone; but, on the other hand, if an action can have both pure and empirical grounds, which grounds were the determining ones (pure or empirical)? Kant calls this a question of transcendental freedom, and much of the "analytic" of the *Critique of Practical Reason* is devoted to it. His solution is to say that for practical purposes one can be sure *that* he is free, but one cannot fully grasp cognitively *how* transcendental freedom is possible. One knows that he can act autonomously, and thereby is the categorical imperative vindicated as a guide for action; but since knowledge (cognition) is a manifestation of the transcendental autonomy of intelligence, he cannot rise to a higher vantage point in order to attain a full cognitive grasp of the ultimate grounds of both knowledge and action.

All of the foregoing topics that are treated in the *Grounding* and the *Critique* are preparation for the systematic presentation of doctrine in the *Metaphysics of Morals*, which has two parts called respectively *The Metaphysical Principles of Right* (jurisprudence) and *The Metaphysical Principles of Virtue* (ethics).[1] Today many philosophers would call Kant's treatment of the foundations and method of morals as contained in the *Grounding* and *Critique* "meta-ethical" and the doctrine of the *Metaphysics of Morals* his "normative ethics." This is a good way to emphasize again that the former two treatises are slanted in the direction of high-level abstractions. People who read mainly the *Grounding* and the *Critique* often criticize Kant for having his head in the clouds and for not being convincingly capable of dealing with concrete cases. A reading of the *Metaphysics of Morals* will show anyone how unfounded such criticisms are.

To be sure, the principle of autonomy (the moral law) as examined in the *Grounding* and justified in the *Critique* is perfectly general and applies to all rational agents as such (to agents who are able to act from reason and not merely from inclinations of sense). Accordingly, the moral law makes no distinctions between God and man. However, duties cannot be ascribed to a perfectly rational agent (God), inasmuch as such an agent always acts in accordance with the moral law because in this case there are no senses involved to incline such a being by means of self-interest to act contrary to the moral law. But in the case of humans, account must be taken of their desires and interests, which may urge action contrary to the moral law. Indeed the relation of human beings to the law is always one of obligation since man has both reason and senses; humans alone have

---

1. For an ingratiating but profoundly penetrating study of the whole system of Kant's moral philosophy (that is as rewarding an introductory study as is to be found anywhere) see Warner Wick's Introduction to *Kant's Ethical Philosophy* (my translation of *Grounding for the Metaphysics of Morals* and *The Metaphysical Principles of Virtue* combined in one volume, published by Hackett, Indianapolis, 1982). I have found many of his thoughts in that essay (especially those in his Section I) quite helpful here in my Introduction to the *Grounding*.

duties. Animals do not act rationally but solely by instinct and sensuous inclinations, and hence have no obligations or duties (man is the only living being that blushes and the only one that needs to).

The concepts of human desire and its many kinds are empirical, to be sure. These empirical concepts in conjunction with the supreme moral principle yield the various classes of specific duties that make up the body of doctrine contained in the *Metaphysics of Morals*. In analogous fashion, the empirically given concept of matter when determined by the transcendental predicates conveyed in the pure categories of the understanding yield the body of doctrine regarding corporeal nature that is contained in the *Metaphysical Foundations of Natural Science*. The empirical concepts of desires and interests are what relate the fundamental law of morality to the human condition. But this use of empirical concepts does not make the propositions of the body of moral metaphysical doctrine empirical in the sense that its propositions are dependent on empirical evidence and are thereby true only contingently. If this were so, then the *Metaphysics of Morals* would contain nothing but hypothetical imperatives; however, it comprises a system of particular categorical imperatives (thou shalt honor contracts, thou shalt not commit suicide, thou shalt not overindulge in food and drink, etc.). Indeed moral philosophy is such that its a priori part exhausts what is called doctrine proper. Moral philosophy does have an empirical part contained in what Kant calls practical anthropology; but the contribution of the latter is merely supplemental, inasmuch as morals are concerned with what should be done rather than with what actually is done. Such anthropology considers, for example, the frequent failure in what should be done and how such mistakes can be avoided in the future. In this respect moral doctrine contrasts with natural doctrine. The empirical laws of nature investigated in empirical physics comprise the largest part of natural science, while the transcendental system of nature contained in the "Analytic of Principles" in the *Critique of Pure Reason* and the metaphysical system of nature contained in the *Metaphysical Foundations of Natural Science* make up but a small—yet important—part of the science of nature.

Kant's approach to moral philosophy involves going from the fundamental principle of autonomy to specific rules of duty (particular categorical imperatives) and finally down to cases. Moral philosophy is intended for what can be realized in action amid changing circumstances. Kant is often upbraided for having given the world in the instance of the categorical imperative an empty formula with no power for determining rules sufficiently specific for any effective guidance in concrete situations. It is also said that the prescriptions which he does offer are so lacking in flexibility that they do not fit either the changing situations everyone faces or the various values among which one has to choose. Both the *Grounding* and the *Critique* deal primarily with the categorical imperative as a universal principle, but the *Metaphysics of Morals* provides the reader with a better-balanced perspective. Even though this last-mentioned treatise deals mainly with general categories of duties, those duties nevertheless are oriented toward concrete action; and in the *Metaphysical Principles of Virtue* the reader will even find sections devoted to casuistical questions. For example, in the days before anti-rabies serum would a man bitten by a mad dog do wrong to commit suicide lest in his final raving sickness he might himself uncontrollably bite someone? Obviously the maxim upon which he acted would be quite different from that of someone who threw himself out of a high window upon learning that he had been financially wiped out in the 1929 stock market crash.

The field of the moral law's legislation has two main subdivisions. The first one is the domain of justice and legality, and Kant calls this one the domain of right (*Recht*); accordingly, the first part of the *Metaphysics of Morals* is called the *Metaphysical Principles of the Doctrine of Right*. The second one is the domain of virtue (*Tugend*), and the second part is called the *Metaphysical Principles of the Doctrine of Virtue*. To pay or not to pay one's debts, to respect or violate somebody's rights are matters of justice or injustice that can be rewarded or punished. But virtue or vice, merit or depravity are internal and personal things that are out of reach of the law.

Kant distinguishes legality and morality quite succinctly in terms of the concept of legislation, which involves a rule to be followed and an incentive for following it. Ethical legislation makes something a duty and declares that the appropriate reason for fulfilling that duty is the very fact that the something under consideration is a duty, e.g., no one can be compelled by law to be beneficent (though he may be taxed and this money then distributed in welfare payments), but if someone is beneficent, this beneficence is its own reason for being. In the case of juridical legislation, rewards and punishments are attached as incentives to the fulfillment of the duties involved, e.g., if one does not pay his taxes, he will be fined. Ethical legislation is internal, while the juridical is external. Jurisprudence is the science of external legislation, and the supreme principle of right says that one should act externally in such a way that the free use of one's choice may not interfere with anyone's freedom insofar as his freedom agrees with universal law.

Ethical obligations are discharged only when they are done out of respect for the law; such performance involves merit over and above merely being free from blame. All juridical duties when done for duty's sake (and not merely for some reward or the avoidance of punishment) are thereby ethical duties. But there is a second kind of ethical duty called duties of virtue. These are the ones which are considered in the *Metaphysical Principles of Virtue*, and are those for which no external legislation is possible; they include such duties as not to commit suicide, not to overindulge in food and drink, not to lie, not to become anyone's doormat, to be beneficent, grateful, sympathetic, not to be prideful, full of calumny, full of mockery, and yet others.

It is not the intention of this introduction to provide the reader with a bird's-eye view of the *Metaphysics of Morals* (which is longer than the *Grounding* and the *Critique* combined). I have intended merely to give enough information about the *Metaphysics of Morals* to impress upon the reader that he cannot get a balanced impression of Kant's conception of moral philosophy by considering only the *Grounding* and the *Critique*. Also he cannot fully grasp the *Metaphysics of Morals* without first studying the other two treatises, especially the *Grounding*.

Kant's treatment of moral philosophy is a profound—and lengthy— affair; and most certainly the only place to start is with the *Grounding*, which lies just ahead. And heaven help the one who enters thereon! Why do I say this? There are two main reasons. First, Kant writes for a rather sophisticated audience. He assumes readers who are well on their way toward rational knowledge. He supposes that they have a rudimentary grasp of the basic points and do not need to have the consequences of those points elaborated in detail. For example, he says that there is one categorical imperative, which can be formulated in five different ways. Yet he does not provide the reader much help in seeing how those formulations are equivalent—in fact several generations of students and commentators have been confused on this point, including John Stuart Mill. Second, he has such a firm grip on his material that he does not always judge wisely as to where the reader may stand in need of extra help if he is not to go astray. But, students, be of good cheer! Your teachers, one hopes, will be able to lead you through the maze. If they falter, consult the ensuing Selected Bibliography for further help. And never forget that struggling with Kant (or any other great but difficult philosopher) can be very rewarding.

SELECTED BIBLIOGRAPHY

The literature devoted to the *Grounding* and to various aspects thereof is enormous. The following list includes only works written in English which have appeared in the recent past.

Duncan, A. R. C. *Practical Reason and Morality. A Study of Immanuel Kant's Foundations for the Metaphysics of Morals.* (Edinburgh, 1957.)

Paton, H. J. *The Categorical Imperative. A Study in Kant's Moral Philosophy.* (London, 1947).

_____. *The Moral Law. Kant's Groundwork of the Metaphysics of Morals.* (London, 1948).

Wolff, Robert Paul. *The Autonomy of Reason. A Commentary on Kant's Groundwork of the Metaphysics of Morals.* (New York, 1973).

_____. *Foundations of the Metaphysics of Morals with Critical Essays* (ed. R. P. Wolff). (Indianapolis, 1969).

Grundlegung

zur

Metaphysik

der Sitten

von

Immanuel Kant.

Riga,

bey Johann Friedrich Hartknoch.

1785.

Ancient Greek philosophy was divided into three sciences: physics, ethics, and logic. This division is perfectly suitable to the nature of the subject, and the only improvement that can be made in it is perhaps only to supply its principle so that there will be a possibility on the one hand of insuring its completeness and on the other of correctly determining its necessary subdivisions.

All rational knowledge is either material and concerned with some object, or formal and concerned only with the form of understanding and of reason themselves and with the universal rules of thought in general without regard to differences of its objects. Formal philosophy is called logic. Material philosophy, however, has to do with determinate objects and with the laws to which these objects are subject; and such philosophy is divided into two parts, because these laws are either laws of nature or laws of freedom. The science of the former is called physics, while that of the latter is called ethics; they are also called doctrine of nature and doctrine of morals respectively.

Logic cannot have any empirical part, i.e., a part in which the universal and necessary laws of thought would be based on grounds taken from experience; for in that case it would not be logic, i.e., a canon for understanding and reason, which is valid for all thinking and which has to be demonstrated.[1] Natural and moral philosophy, on the contrary, can each have an empirical part. The former has to because it must determine the laws of nature as an object of experience, and the latter because it must determine the will of man insofar as the will is affected by nature. The laws of the former are those according to which everything does happen, while the laws of the latter are those according to which everything ought to happen, although these moral laws also consider the conditions under which what ought to happen frequently does not.

All philosophy insofar as it is founded on experience may be called empirical, while that which sets forth its doctrines as founded entirely on a priori principles may be called pure. The latter, when merely formal, is called logic; but when limited to determinate objects of the understanding, it is called metaphysics.

In this way there arises the idea of a twofold metaphysics: a metaphysics of nature and a metaphysics of morals.[2] Physics will thus

1. [Kant's *Logic* was first published in 1800 in a version edited by Gottlob Benjamin Jäsche, who was one of Kant's students.]

2. [*The Metaphysical Foundations of Natural Science* was published in 1786. *The Metaphysics of Morals* appeared in 1797.]

have its empirical part, but also a rational one. Ethics will too, though here the empirical part might more specifically be called practical anthropology,[3] while the rational part might properly be called morals.

All industries, crafts, and arts have gained by the division of labor, viz., one man does not do everything, but each confines himself to a certain kind of work that is distinguished from all other kinds by the treatment it requires, so that the work may be done with the highest perfection and with greater ease. Where work is not so distinguished and divided, where everyone is a jack of all trades, there industry remains sunk in the greatest barbarism. Whether or not pure philosophy in all its parts requires its own special man might well be in itself a subject worthy of consideration. Would not the whole of this learned industry be better off if those who are accustomed, as the public taste demands, to purvey a mixture of the empirical with the rational in all sorts of proportions unknown even to themselves and who style themselves independent thinkers, while giving the name of hair-splitters to those who apply themselves to the purely rational part, were to be given warning about pursuing simultaneously two jobs which are quite different in their technique, and each of which perhaps requires a special talent that when combined with the other talent produces nothing but bungling? But I only ask here whether the nature of science does not require that the empirical part always be carefully separated from the rational part. Should not physics proper (i.e., empirical physics) be preceded by a metaphysics of nature, and practical anthropology by a metaphysics of morals? Both of these 389 metaphysics must be carefully purified of everything empirical in order to know how much pure reason can accomplish in each case and from what sources it draws its a priori teaching, whether such teaching be conducted by all moralists (whose name is legion) or only by some who feel a calling thereto.

Since I am here primarily concerned with moral philosophy, the foregoing question will be limited to a consideration of whether or not there is the utmost necessity for working out for once a pure moral philosophy that is wholly cleared of everything which can only be empirical and can only belong to anthropology. That there must be such a philosophy is evident from the common idea of duty and of moral laws. Everyone must admit that if a law is to be morally valid, i.e., is to be valid as a ground of obligation, then it must carry with it absolute necessity. He must admit that the command, "Thou shalt not lie," does not hold only for men, as if other rational beings had no need to abide by it, and so with all the other moral laws properly so called. And he must concede that the ground of obligation here must therefore be sought not in the nature of man nor in the circumstances of the world in which man is placed, but must be sought a priori solely in the concepts of pure reason; he must grant that every other precept which is founded on principles of mere experience—even a precept that may in certain respects be universal—

---

3. [*Anthropology from a Pragmatic Point of View* first appeared in 1798.]

insofar as it rests in the least on empirical grounds—perhaps only in its motive—can indeed be called a practical rule, but never a moral law.

Thus not only are moral laws together with their principles essentially different from every kind of practical cognition in which there is anything empirical, but all moral philosophy rests entirely on its pure part. When applied to man, it does not in the least borrow from acquaintance with him (anthropology) but gives a priori laws to him as a rational being. To be sure, these laws require, furthermore, a power of judgment sharpened by experience, partly in order to distinguish in what cases they are applicable, and partly to gain for them access to the human will as well as influence for putting them into practice. For man is affected by so many inclinations that, even though he is indeed capable of the idea of a pure practical reason, he is not so easily able to make that idea effective *in concreto* in the conduct of his life.

A metaphysics of morals is thus indispensably necessary, not merely because of motives of speculation regarding the source of practical principles which are present a priori in our reason, but because morals themselves are liable to all kinds of corruption as long as the guide and supreme norm for correctly estimating them are missing. For in the case of what is to be morally good, that it conforms to the moral law is not enough; it must also be done for the sake of the moral law. Otherwise that conformity is only very contingent and uncertain, since the non-moral ground may now and then produce actions that conform with the law but quite often produces actions that are contrary to the law. Now the moral law in its purity and genuineness (which is of the utmost concern in the practical realm) can be sought nowhere but in a pure philosophy. Therefore, pure philosophy (metaphysics) must precede; without it there can be no moral philosophy at all. That philosophy which mixes pure principles with empirical ones does not deserve the name of philosophy (for philosophy is distinguished from ordinary rational knowledge by its treatment in a separate science of what the latter comprehends only confusedly). Still less does it deserve the name of moral philosophy, since by this very confusion it spoils even the purity of morals and counteracts its own end.

There must be no thought that what is required here is already contained in the propaedeutic that precedes the celebrated Wolff's moral philosophy, i.e., in what he calls *Universal Practical Philosophy*,[4] and that hence there is no need to break entirely new ground. Just because his work was to be a universal practical philosophy, it has not taken into consideration any special kind of will, such as one determined solely by a priori principles without any empirical motives and which could be called a pure will, but has considered volition in general, together with all the

390

4.[This work of Christian Wolff was published in 1738–39; this and other of his works served for many years as the standard philosophy textbooks in German universities. Wolff's philosophy was founded on that of Leibniz.]

actions and conditions belonging to it under this general signification. And thereby does his propaedeutic differ from a metaphysics of morals in the same way that general logic, which expounds the acts and rules of thinking in general, differs from transcendental philosophy, which treats merely of the particular acts and rules of pure thinking, i.e., of that thinking whereby objects are cognized completely a priori. For the metaphysics of morals has to investigate the idea and principles of a possible pure will and not the actions and conditions of human volition as such, which are

391 for the most part drawn from psychology. Moral laws and duty are discussed in this universal practical philosophy (though quite improperly), but this is no objection to what has been said about such philosophy. For the authors of this science remain true to their idea of it on the following point also: they do not distinguish the motives which, as such, are presented completely a priori by reason alone and are properly moral from the empirical motives which the understanding raises to general concepts merely by the comparison of experiences. Rather, they consider motives irrespective of any difference in their source; and inasmuch as they regard all motives as being homogeneous, they consider nothing but their relative strength or weakness. In this way they frame their concept of obligation, which is certainly not moral, but is all that can be expected from a philosophy which never decides regarding the origin of all possible practical concepts whether they are a priori or merely a posteriori.

I intend some day to publish a metaphysics of morals,[5] but as a preliminary to that I now issue this *Grounding* [1785]. Indeed there is properly no other foundation for such a metaphysics than a critical examination of pure practical reason, just as there is properly no other foundation for a metaphysics [of nature] than the critical examination of pure speculative reason, which has already been published.[6] But, in the first place, the former critique is not so absolutely necessary as the latter one, because human reason can, even in the most ordinary mind, be easily brought in moral matters to a high degree of correctness and precision, while on the other hand in its theoretical but pure use it is wholly dialectical. In the second place, if a critical examination of pure practical reason is to be complete, then there must, in my view, be the possibility at the same time of showing the unity of practical and speculative reason in a common principle; for in the final analysis there can be only one and the same reason, which is to be differentiated solely in its application. But there is no possibility here of bringing my work to such completeness, without introducing considerations of an entirely different kind and without thereby confusing the reader. Instead of calling the present work a *Critique of Pure Practical Reason*, I have, therefore, adopted the title

5. [This appeared in 1797.]

6. [The first edition of the *Critique of Pure Reason* appeared in 1781, while the second edition appeared in 1787. The *Critique of Practical Reason* was published in 1788.]

Grounding for the Metaphysics of Morals [*Grundlegung zur Metaphysik der Sitten.*][7]

But, in the third place, since a metaphysics of morals, despite the forbidding title, is nevertheless capable of a high degree of popularity and adaptation to the ordinary understanding, I find it useful to separate from the aforementioned metaphysics this preliminary work on its foundation [*Grundlage*] in order later to have no need to introduce unavoidable subtleties into doctrines that are easier to grasp.

392

The present *Grounding* [*Grundlegung*] is, however, intended for nothing more than seeking out and establishing the supreme principle of morality. This constitutes by itself a task which is complete in its purpose and should be kept separate from every other moral inquiry. The application of this supreme principle to the whole ethical system would, to be sure, shed much light on my conclusions regarding this central question, which is important but has not heretofore been at all satisfactorily discussed; and the adequacy manifested by the principle throughout such application would provide strong confirmation for the principle. Nevertheless, I must forego this advantage, which after all would be more gratifying for myself than helpful for others, since ease of use and apparent adequacy of a principle do not provide any certain proof of its soundness, but do awaken, rather, a certain bias which prevents any rigorous examination and estimation of it for itself without any regard to its consequences.

The method adopted in this work is, I believe, one that is most suitable if we proceed analytically from ordinary knowledge to a determination of the supreme principle and then back again synthetically from an examination of this principle and its sources to ordinary knowledge where its application is found. Therefore, the division turns out to be the following:

1. First Section.   Transition from the Ordinary Rational Knowledge of Morality to the Philosophical

2. Second Section.   Transition from Popular Moral Philosophy to a Metaphysics of Morals

3. Third Section.   Final Step from a Metaphysics of Morals to a Critique of Pure Practical Reason.

7. [This might be translated as *Laying the Foundation for the Metaphysics of Morals.* But for the sake of brevity *Grounding for the Metaphysics of Morals* has been chosen.]

TRANSITION FROM THE ORDINARY RATIONAL KNOWLEDGE
OF MORALITY TO THE PHILOSOPHICAL

There is no possibility of thinking of anything at all in the world, or even out of it, which can be regarded as good without qualification, except a *good will.* Intelligence, wit, judgment, and whatever talents of the mind one might want to name are doubtless in many respects good and desirable, as are such qualities of temperament as courage, resolution, perseverance. But they can also become extremely bad and harmful if the will, which is to make use of these gifts of nature and which in its special constitution is called character, is not good. The same holds with gifts of fortune; power, riches, honor, even health, and that complete well-being and contentment with one's condition which is called happiness make for pride and often hereby even arrogance, unless there is a good will to correct their influence on the mind and herewith also to rectify the whole principle of action and make it universally conformable to its end. The sight of a being who is not graced by any touch of a pure and good will but who yet enjoys an uninterrupted prosperity can never delight a rational and impartial spectator. Thus a good will seems to constitute the indispensable condition of being even worthy of happiness.

Some qualities are even conducive to this good will itself and can facilitate its work. Nevertheless, they have no intrinsic unconditional 394 worth; but they always presuppose, rather, a good will, which restricts the high esteem in which they are otherwise rightly held, and does not permit them to be regarded as absolutely good. Moderation in emotions and passions, self-control, and calm deliberation are not only good in many respects but even seem to constitute part of the intrinsic worth of a person. But they are far from being rightly called good without qualification (however unconditionally they were commended by the ancients). For without the principles of a good will, they can become extremely bad; the coolness of a villain makes him not only much more dangerous but also immediately more abominable in our eyes than he would have been regarded by us without it.

A good will is good not because of what it effects or accomplishes, nor because of its fitness to attain some proposed end; it is good only through its willing, i.e., it is good in itself. When it is considered in itself, then it is to be esteemed very much higher than anything which it might ever bring about merely in order to favor some inclination, or even the sum total of all inclinations. Even if, by some especially unfortunate fate or by the nig-

7

gardly provision of stepmotherly nature, this will should be wholly lacking in the power to accomplish its purpose; if with the greatest effort it
should yet achieve nothing, and only the good will should remain (not, to
be sure, as a mere wish but as the summoning of all the means in our
power), yet would it, like a jewel, still shine by its own light as something
which has its full value in itself. Its usefulness or fruitlessness can neither
augment nor diminish this value. Its usefulness would be, as it were, only
the setting to enable us to handle it in ordinary dealings or to attract to it
the attention of those who are not yet experts, but not to recommend it to
real experts or to determine its value.

But there is something so strange in this idea of the absolute value of a
mere will, in which no account is taken of any useful results, that in spite
of all the agreement received even from ordinary reason, yet there must
arise the suspicion that such an idea may perhaps have as its hidden basis
merely some high-flown fancy, and that we may have misunderstood the
395   purpose of nature in assigning to reason the governing of our will.
Therefore, this idea will be examined from this point of view.

In the natural constitution of an organized being, i.e., one suitably
adapted to the purpose of life, let us take as a principle that in such a
being no organ is to be found for any end unless it be the most fit and the
best adapted for that end. Now if that being's preservation, welfare, or in
a word its happiness, were the real end of nature in the case of a being
having reason and will, then nature would have hit upon a very poor arrangement in having the reason of the creature carry out this purpose. For
all the actions which such a creature has to perform with this purpose in
view, and the whole rule of his conduct would have been prescribed
much more exactly by instinct; and the purpose in question could have
been attained much more certainly by instinct than it ever can be by
reason. And if in addition reason had been imparted to this favored
creature, then it would have had to serve him only to contemplate the
happy constitution of his nature, to admire that nature, to rejoice in it,
and to feel grateful to the cause that bestowed it; but reason would not
have served him to subject his faculty of desire to its weak and delusive
guidance nor would it have served him to meddle incompetently with the
purpose of nature. In a word, nature would have taken care that reason
did not strike out into a practical use nor presume, with its weak insight,
to think out for itself a plan for happiness and the means for attaining it.
Nature would have taken upon herself not only the choice of ends but also
that of the means, and would with wise foresight have entrusted both to
instinct alone.

And, in fact, we find that the more a cultivated reason devotes itself to
the aim of enjoying life and happiness, the further does man get away
from true contentment. Because of this there arises in many persons, if
only they are candid enough to admit it, a certain degree of misology,
i.e., hatred of reason. This is especially so in the case of those who are the
most experienced in the use of reason, because after calculating all the advantages they derive, I say not from the invention of all the arts of com-

mon luxury, but even from the sciences (which in the end seem to them to be also a luxury of the understanding), they yet find that they have in fact only brought more trouble on their heads than they have gained in happiness. Therefore, they come to envy, rather than despise, the more common run of men who are closer to the guidance of mere natural instinct and who do not allow their reason much influence on their conduct. And we must admit that the judgment of those who would temper, or even reduce below zero, the boastful eulogies on behalf of the advantages which reason is supposed to provide as regards the happiness and contentment of life is by no means morose or ungrateful to the goodness with which the world is governed. There lies at the root of such judgments, rather, the idea that existence has another and much more worthy purpose, for which, and not for happiness, reason is quite properly intended, and which must, therefore, be regarded as the supreme condition to which the private purpose of men must, for the most part, defer.

Reason, however, is not competent enough to guide the will safely as regards its objects and the satisfaction of all our needs (which it in part even multiplies); to this end would an implanted natural instinct have led much more certainly. But inasmuch as reason has been imparted to us as a practical faculty, i.e., as one which is to have influence on the will, its true function must be to produce a will which is not merely good as a means to some further end, but is good in itself. To produce a will good in itself reason was absolutely necessary, inasmuch as nature in distributing her capacities has everywhere gone to work in a purposive manner. While such a will may not indeed be the sole and complete good, it must, nevertheless, be the highest good and the condition of all the rest, even of the desire for happiness. In this case there is nothing inconsistent with the wisdom of nature that the cultivation of reason, which is requisite for the first and unconditioned purpose, may in many ways restrict, at least in this life, the attainment of the second purpose, viz., happiness, which is always conditioned. Indeed happiness can even be reduced to less than nothing, without nature's failing thereby in her purpose; for reason recognizes as its highest practical function the establishment of a good will, whereby in the attainment of this end reason is capable only of its own kind of satisfaction, viz., that of fulfilling a purpose which is in turn determined only by reason, even though such fulfilment were often to interfere with the purposes of inclination.

The concept of a will estimable in itself and good without regard to any further end must now be developed. This concept already dwells in the natural sound understanding and needs not so much to be taught as merely to be elucidated. It always holds first place in estimating the total worth of our actions and constitutes the condition of all the rest. Therefore, we shall take up the concept of *duty*, which includes that of a good will, though with certain subjective restrictions and hindrances, which far from hiding a good will or rendering it unrecognizable, rather bring it out by contrast and make it shine forth more brightly.

I here omit all actions already recognized as contrary to duty, even though they may be useful for this or that end; for in the case of these the question does not arise at all as to whether they might be done from duty, since they even conflict with duty. I also set aside those actions which are really in accordance with duty, yet to which men have no immediate inclination, but perform them because they are impelled thereto by some other inclination. For in this [second] case to decide whether the action which is in accord with duty has been done from duty or from some selfish purpose is easy. This difference is far more difficult to note in the [third] case where the action accords with duty and the subject has in addition an immediate inclination to do the action. For example,[1] that a dealer should not overcharge an inexperienced purchaser certainly accords with duty; and where there is much commerce, the prudent merchant does not overcharge but keeps to a fixed price for everyone in general, so that a child may buy from him just as well as everyone else may. Thus customers are honestly served, but this is not nearly enough for making us believe that the merchant has acted this way from duty and from principles of honesty; his own advantage required him to do it. He cannot, however, be assumed to have in addition [as in the third case] an immediate inclination toward his buyers, causing him, as it were, out of love to give no one as far as price is concerned any advantage over another. Hence the action was done neither from duty nor from immediate inclination, but merely for a selfish purpose.

398   On the other hand,[2] to preserve one's life is a duty; and, furthermore, everyone has also an immediate inclination to do so. But on this account the often anxious care taken by most men for it has no intrinsic worth, and the maxim of their action has no moral content. They preserve their lives, to be sure, in accordance with duty, but not from duty. On the other hand,[3] if adversity and hopeless sorrow have completely taken away the taste for life, if an unfortunate man, strong in soul and more indignant at his fate than despondent or dejected, wishes for death and yet preserves his life without loving it—not from inclination or fear, but from duty—then his maxim indeed has a moral content.[4]

1. [The ensuing example provides an illustration of the second case.]

2. [This next example illustrates the third case.]

3. [The ensuing example illustrates the fourth case.]

4. [Four different cases have been distinguished in the two foregoing paragraphs. Case 1 involves those actions which are contrary to duty (lying, cheating, stealing, etc.). Case 2 involves those which accord with duty but for which a person perhaps has no immediate inclination, though he does have a mediate inclination thereto (one pays his taxes not because he likes to but in order to avoid the penalties set for delinquents, one treats his fellows well not because he really likes them but because he wants their votes when at some future time he runs for public office, etc.). A vast number of so-called "morally good" actions actually belong to this case 2—they accord with duty because of self-seeking inclinations. Case 3 involves those which accord with duty and for which a person does have an immediate inclination (one does not commit suicide because all is going well with him, one does not commit adultery because he considers his wife to be the most desirable creature in the whole world,

To be beneficent where one can is a duty; and besides this, there are many persons who are so sympathetically constituted that, without any further motive of vanity or self-interest, they find an inner pleasure in spreading joy around them and can rejoice in the satisfaction of others as their own work. But I maintain that in such a case an action of this kind, however dutiful and amiable it may be, has nevertheless no true moral worth.[5] It is on a level with such actions as arise from other inclinations, e.g., the inclination for honor, which if fortunately directed to what is in fact beneficial and accords with duty and is thus honorable, deserves praise and encouragement, but not esteem; for its maxim lacks the moral content of an action done not from inclination but from duty. Suppose then the mind of this friend of mankind to be clouded over with his own sorrow so that all sympathy with the lot of others is extinguished, and suppose him still to have the power to benefit others in distress, even though he is not touched by their trouble because he is sufficiently absorbed with his own; and now suppose that, even though no inclination moves him any longer, he nevertheless tears himself from this deadly insensibility and performs the action without any inclination at all, but solely from duty—then for the first time his action has genuine moral worth.[6] Further still, if nature has put little sympathy in this or that man's heart, if (while being an honest man in other respects) he is by temperament cold and indifferent to the sufferings of others, perhaps because as regards his own sufferings he is endowed with the special gift of patience and fortitude and expects or even requires that others should have the same; if such a man (who would truly not be nature's worst product) had not been exactly fashioned by her to be a philanthropist, would he not yet find in himself a source from which he might give himself a worth far higher than any that a good-natured temperament might have? By all means, because just here

---

etc.). Case 4 involves those actions which accord with duty but are contary to some immediate inclination (one does not commit suicide even when he is in dire distress, one does not commit adultery even though his wife has turned out to be an impossible shrew, etc.). Now case 4 is the crucial test case of the will's possible goodness—but Kant does not claim that one should lead his life in such a way as to encounter as many such cases as possible in order constantly to test his virtue (deliberately marry a shrew so as to be able to resist the temptation to commit adultery). Life itself forces enough such cases upon a person without his seeking them out. But when there is a conflict between duty and inclination, duty should always be followed. Case 3 makes for the easiest living and the greatest contentment, and anyone would wish that life might present him with far more of these cases than with cases 2 or 4. But yet one should not arrange his life in such a way as to avoid case 4 at all costs and to seek out case 3 as much as possible (become a recluse so as to avoid the possible rough and tumble involved with frequent association with one's fellows, avoid places where one might encounter the sick and the poor so as to spare oneself the pangs of sympathy and the need to exercise the virtue of benefiting those in distress, etc.). For the purpose of philosophical analysis Kant emphasizes case 4 as being the test case of the will's possible goodness, but he is not thereby advocating puritanism.]

5. [This is an example of case 3.]

6. [This is an example of case 4.]

399   does the worth of the character come out; this worth is moral and incomparably the highest of all, viz., that he is beneficent, not from inclination, but from duty.[7]

To secure one's own happiness is a duty (at least indirectly); for discontent with one's condition under many pressing cares and amid unsatisfied wants might easily become a great temptation to transgress one's duties. But here also do men of themselves already have, irrespective of duty, the strongest and deepest inclination toward happiness, because just in this idea are all inclinations combined into a sum total.[8] But the precept of happiness is often so constituted as greatly to interfere with some inclinations, and yet men cannot form any definite and certain concept of the sum of satisfaction of all inclinations that is called happiness. Hence there is no wonder that a single inclination which is determinate both as to what it promises and as to the time within which it can be satisfied may outweigh a fluctuating idea; and there is no wonder that a man, e.g., a gouty patient, can choose to enjoy what he likes and to suffer what he may, since by his calculation he has here at least not sacrificed the enjoyment of the present moment to some possibly groundless expectations of the good fortune that is supposed to be found in health. But even in this case, if the universal inclination to happiness did not determine his will and if health, at least for him, did not figure as so necessary an element in his calculations; there still remains here, as in all other cases, a law, viz., that he should promote his happiness not from inclination but from duty, and thereby for the first time does his conduct have real moral worth.[9]

Undoubtedly in this way also are to be understood those passages of Scripture which command us to love our neighbor and even our enemy. For love as an inclination cannot be commanded; but beneficence from duty, when no inclination impels us[10] and even when a natural and unconquerable aversion opposes such beneficence,[11] is practical, and not pathological, love. Such love resides in the will and not in the propensities of feeling, in principles of action and not in tender sympathy; and only this practical love can be commanded.

The second proposition[12] is this: An action done from duty has its moral worth, not in the purpose that is to be attained by it, but in the maxim ac-

---

7. [This is an even more extreme example of case 4.]

8. [This is an example of case 3.]

9. [This example is a weak form of case 4; the action accords with duty but is not contrary to some immediate inclination.]

10. [This is case 4 in its weak form.]

11. [This is case 4 in its strong form.]

12. [The first proposition of morality says that an action must be done from duty in order to have any moral worth. It is implicit in the preceding examples but was never explicitly stated.]

cording to which the action is determined. The moral worth depends, therefore, not on the realization of the object of the action, but merely on 400 the principle of volition according to which, without regard to any objects of the faculty of desire, the action has been done. From what has gone before it is clear that the purposes which we may have in our actions, as well as their effects regarded as ends and incentives of the will, cannot give to actions any unconditioned and moral worth. Where, then, can this worth lie if it is not to be found in the will's relation to the expected effect? Nowhere but in the principle of the will, with no regard to the ends that can be brought about through such action. For the will stands, as it were, at a crossroads between its a priori principle, which is formal, and its a posteriori incentive, which is material; and since it must be determined by something, it must be determined by the formal principle of volition, if the action is done from duty—and in that case every material principle is taken away from it.

The third proposition, which follows from the other two, can be expressed thus: Duty is the necessity of an action done out of respect for the law. I can indeed have an inclination for an object as the effect of my proposed action; but I can never have respect for such an object, just because it is merely an effect and is not an activity of the will. Similarly, I can have no respect for inclination as such, whether my own or that of another. I can at most, if my own inclination, approve it; and, if that of another, even love it, i.e., consider it to be favorable to my own advantage. An object of respect can only be what is connected with my will solely as ground and never as effect—something that does not serve my inclination but, rather, outweighs it, or at least excludes it from consideration when some choice is made—in other words, only the law itself can be an object of respect and hence can be a command. Now an action done from duty must altogether exclude the influence of inclination and therewith every object of the will. Hence there is nothing left which can determine the will except objectively the law and subjectively pure respect for this practical law, i.e., the will can be subjectively determined by the maxim[13] that I should follow such a law even if all my inclinations are thereby thwarted.   401

Thus the moral worth of an action does not lie in the effect expected from it nor in any principle of action that needs to borrow its motive from this expected effect. For all these effects (agreeableness of one's condition and even the furtherance of other people's happiness) could have been brought about also through other causes and would not have required the will of a rational being, in which the highest and unconditioned good can alone be found. Therefore, the pre-eminent good which is called moral can consist in nothing but the representation of the law in itself, and such a representation can admittedly be found only in a rational being insofar as this representation, and not some expected effect, is the determining

13. A maxim is the subjective principle of volition. The objective principle (i.e., one which would serve all rational beings also subjectively as a practical principle if reason had full control over the faculty of desire) is the practical law. [See below Kant's footnote at Ak. 420–21.]

ground of the will. This good is already present in the person who acts according to this representation, and such good need not be awaited merely from the effect.[14]

402   But what sort of law can that be the thought of which must determine the will without reference to any expected effect, so that the will can be called absolutely good without qualification? Since I have deprived the will of every impulse that might arise for it from obeying any particular law, there is nothing left to serve the will as principle except the universal conformity of its actions to law as such, i.e., I should never act except in such a way that I can also will that my maxim should become a universal law.[15] Here mere conformity to law as such (without having as its basis any law determining particular actions) serves the will as principle and must so serve it if duty is not to be a vain delusion and a chimerical concept. The ordinary reason of mankind in its practical judgments agrees completely with this, and always has in view the aforementioned principle.

For example, take this question. When I am in distress, may I make a promise with the intention of not keeping it? I readily distinguish here the two meanings which the question may have; whether making a false promise conforms with prudence or with duty. Doubtless the former can often be the case. Indeed I clearly see that escape from some present difficulty by means of such a promise is not enough. In addition I must carefully consider whether from this lie there may later arise far greater inconvenience for me than from what I now try to escape. Furthermore, the consequences of my false promise are not easy to forsee, even with all my supposed cunning; loss of confidence in me might prove to be far more disadvantageous than the misfortune which I now try to avoid. The more

14. There might be brought against me here an objection that I take refuge behind the word "respect" in an obscure feeling, instead of giving a clear answer to the question by means of a concept of reason. But even though respect is a feeling, it is not one received through any outside influence but is, rather, one that is self-produced by means of a rational concept; hence it is specifically different from all feelings of the first kind, which can all be reduced to inclination or fear. What I recognize immediately as a law for me, I recognize with respect; this means merely the consciousness of the subordination of my will to a law without the mediation of other influences upon my sense. The immediate determination of the will by the law, and the consciousness thereof, is called respect, which is hence regarded as the effect of the law upon the subject and not as the cause of the law. Respect is properly the representation of a worth that thwarts my self-love. Hence respect is something that is regarded as an object of neither inclination nor fear, although it has at the same time something analogous to both. The object of respect is, therefore, nothing but the law—indeed that very law which we impose on ourselves and yet recognize as necessary in itself. As law, we are subject to it without consulting self-love; as imposed on us by ourselves, it is a consequence of our will. In the former aspect, it is analogous to fear; in the latter, to inclination. All respect for a person is properly only respect for the law (of honesty, etc.) of which the person provides an example. Since we regard the development of our talents as a duty, we think of a man of talent as being also a kind of example of the law (the law of becoming like him by practice), and that is what constitutes our respect for him. All so-called moral interest consists solely in respect for the law.

15. [This is the first time in the *Grounding* that the categorical imperative is stated.]

prudent way might be to act according to a universal maxim and to make it a habit not to promise anything without intending to keep it. But that such a maxim is, nevertheless, always based on nothing but a fear of consequences becomes clear to me at once. To be truthful from duty is, however, quite different from being truthful from fear of disadvantageous consequences; in the first case the concept of the action itself contains a law for me, while in the second I must first look around elsewhere to see what are the results for me that might be connected with the action. For to deviate from the principle of duty is quite certainly bad; but to   403 abandon my maxim of prudence can often be very advantageous for me, though to abide by it is certainly safer. The most direct and infallible way, however, to answer the question as to whether a lying promise accords with duty is to ask myself whether I would really be content if my maxim (of extricating myself from difficulty by means of a false promise) were to hold as a universal law for myself as well as for others, and could I really say to myself that everyone may promise falsely when he finds himself in a difficulty from which he can find no other way to extricate himself. Then I immediately become aware that I can indeed will the lie but can not at all will a universal law to lie. For by such a law there would really be no promises at all, since in vain would my willing future actions be professed to other people who would not believe what I professed, or if they over-hastily did believe, then they would pay me back in like coin. Therefore, my maxim would necessarily destroy itself just as soon as it was made a universal law.[16]

Therefore, I need no far-reaching acuteness to discern what I have to do in order that my will may be morally good. Inexperienced in the course of the world and incapable of being prepared for all its contingencies, I only ask myself whether I can also will that my maxim should become a universal law. If not, then the maxim must be rejected, not because of any disadvantage accruing to me or even to others, but because it cannot be fitting as a principle in a possible legislation of universal law, and reason exacts from me immediate respect for such legislation. Indeed I have as yet no insight into the grounds of such respect (which the philosopher may investigate). But I at least understand that respect is an estimation of a worth that far outweighs any worth of what is recommended by inclination, and that the necessity of acting from pure respect for the practical law is what constitutes duty, to which every other motive must give way because duty is the condition of a will good in itself, whose worth is above all else.

Thus within the moral cognition of ordinary human reason we have arrived at its principle. To be sure, such reason does not think of this principle abstractly in its universal form, but does always have it actually in view and does use it as the standard of judgment. It would here be easy to   404

16. [This means that when you tell a lie, you merely take exception to the general rule that says everyone should always tell the truth and believe that what you are saying is true. When you lie, you do not thereby will that everyone else lie and not believe that what you are saying is true, because in such a case your lie would never work to get you what you want.]

show how ordinary reason, with this compass in hand, is well able to distinguish, in every case that occurs, what is good or evil, in accord with duty or contrary to duty, if we do not in the least try to teach reason anything new but only make it attend, as Socrates did, to its own principle—and thereby do we show that neither science nor philosophy is needed in order to know what one must do to be honest and good, and even wise and virtuous. Indeed we might even have conjectured beforehand that cognizance of what every man is obligated to do, and hence also to know, would be available to every man, even the most ordinary. Yet we cannot but observe with admiration how great an advantage the power of practical judgment has over the theoretical in ordinary human understanding. In the theoretical, when ordinary reason ventures to depart from the laws of experience and the perceptions of sense, it falls into sheer inconceivabilities and self-contradictions, or at least into a chaos of uncertainty, obscurity, and instability. In the practical, however, the power of judgment first begins to show itself to advantage when ordinary understanding excludes all sensuous incentives from practical laws. Such understanding then becomes even subtle, whether in quibbling with its own conscience or with other claims regarding what is to be called right, or whether in wanting to determine correctly for its own instruction the worth of various actions. And the most extraordinary thing is that ordinary understanding in this practical case may have just as good a hope of hitting the mark as that which any philosopher may promise himself. Indeed it is almost more certain in this than even a philosopher is, because he can have no principle other than what ordinary understanding has, but he may easily confuse his judgment by a multitude of foreign and irrelevant considerations and thereby cause it to swerve from the right way. Would it not, therefore, be wiser in moral matters to abide by the ordinary rational judgment or at most to bring in philosophy merely for the purpose of rendering the system of morals more complete and intelligible and of presenting its rules in a way that is more convenient for use (especially in disputation), but not for the purpose of leading ordinary human understanding away from its happy simplicity in practical matters and of bringing it by means of philosophy into a new path of inquiry and instruction?

405   Innocence is indeed a glorious thing; but, unfortunately, it does not keep very well and is easily led astray. Consequently, even wisdom—which consists more in doing and not doing than in knowing—needs science, not in order to learn from it, but in order that wisdom's precepts may gain acceptance and permanence. Man feels within himself a powerful counterweight to all the commands of duty, which are presented to him by reason as being so pre-eminently worthy of respect; this counterweight consists of his needs and inclinations, whose total satisfaction is summed up under the name of happiness. Now reason irremissibly commands its precepts, without thereby promising the inclinations anything; hence it disregards and neglects these impetuous and at the same time so seemingly plausible claims (which do not allow themselves to

be suppressed by any command). Hereby arises a natural dialectic, i.e., a propensity to quibble with these strict laws of duty, to cast doubt upon their validity, or at least upon their purity and strictness, and to make them, where possible, more compatible with our wishes and inclinations. Thereby are such laws corrupted in their very foundations and their whole dignity is destroyed—something which even ordinary practical reason cannot in the end call good.

Thus is ordinary human reason forced to go outside its sphere and take a step into the field of practical philosophy, not by any need for speculation (which never befalls such reason so long as it is content to be mere sound reason) but on practical grounds themselves. There it tries to obtain information and clear instruction regarding the source of its own principle and the correct determination of this principle in its opposition to maxims based on need and inclination, so that reason may escape from the perplexity of opposite claims and may avoid the risk of losing all genuine moral principles through the ambiguity into which it easily falls. Thus when ordinary practical reason cultivates itself, there imperceptibly arises in it a dialectic which compels it to seek help in philosophy. The same thing happens in reason's theoretical use; in this case, just as in the other, peace will be found only in a thorough critical examination of our reason.

TRANSITION FROM POPULAR MORAL PHILOSOPHY
TO A METAPHYSICS OF MORALS

If we have so far drawn our concept of duty from the ordinary use of our practical reason, one is by no means to infer that we have treated it as a concept of experience. On the contrary, when we pay attention to our experience of the way human beings act, we meet frequent and—as we ourselves admit—justified complaints that there cannot be cited a single certain example of the disposition to act from pure duty; and we meet complaints that although much may be done that is in accordance with what duty commands, yet there are always doubts as to whether what occurs has really been done from duty and so has moral worth. Hence there have always been philosophers who have absolutely denied the reality of this disposition in human actions and have ascribed everything to a more or less refined self-love. Yet in so doing they have not cast doubt upon the rightness of the concept of morality. Rather, they have spoken with sincere regret as to the frailty and impurity of human nature, which they think is noble enough to take as its precept an idea so worthy of respect but yet is too weak to follow this idea: reason, which should legislate for human nature, is used only to look after the interest of inclinations, whether singly or, at best, in their greatest possible harmony with one another.

In fact there is absolutely no possibility by means of experience to make 407 out with complete certainty a single case in which the maxim of an action that may in other respects conform to duty has rested solely on moral grounds and on the representation of one's duty. It is indeed sometimes the case that after the keenest self-examination we can find nothing except the moral ground of duty that could have been strong enough to move us to this or that good action and to such great sacrifice. But there cannot with certainty be at all inferred from this that some secret impulse of self-love, merely appearing as the idea of duty, was not the actual determining cause of the will. We like to flatter ourselves with the false claim to a more noble motive; but in fact we can never, even by the strictest examination, completely plumb the depths of the secret incentives of our actions. For when moral value is being considered, the concern is not with the actions, which are seen, but rather with their inner principles, which are not seen.

Moreover, one cannot better serve the wishes of those who ridicule all morality as being a mere phantom of human imagination getting above

itself because of self-conceit than by conceding to them that the concepts
of duty must be drawn solely from experience (just as from indolence one
willingly persuades himself that such is the case as regards all other concepts as well). For by so conceding, one prepares for them a sure triumph.
I am willing to admit out of love for humanity that most of our actions are
in accordance with duty; but if we look more closely at our planning and
striving, we everywhere come upon the dear self, which is always turning
up, and upon which the intent of our actions is based rather than upon the
strict command of duty (which would often require self-denial). One need
not be exactly an enemy of virtue, but only a cool observer who does not
take the liveliest wish for the good to be straight off its realization, in
order to become doubtful at times whether any true virtue is actually to
be found in the world. Such is especially the case when years increase and
one's power of judgment is made shrewder by experience and keener in
observation. Because of these things nothing can protect us from a complete falling away from our ideas of duty and preserve in the soul a well-
408   grounded respect for duty's law except the clear conviction that, even if
there never have been actions springing from such pure sources, the question at issue here is not whether this or that has happened but that reason
of itself and independently of all experience commands what ought to
happen. Consequently, reason unrelentingly commands actions of which
the world has perhaps hitherto never provided an example and whose
feasibility might well be doubted by one who bases everything upon experience; for instance, even though there might never yet have been a
sincere friend, still pure sincerity in friendship is nonetheless required of
every man, because this duty, prior to all experience, is contained as duty
in general in the idea of a reason that determines the will by means of a
priori grounds.

There may be noted further that unless we want to deny to the concept
of morality all truth and all reference to a possible object, we cannot but
admit that the moral law is of such widespread significance that it must
hold not merely for men but for all rational beings generally, and that it
must be valid not merely under contingent conditions and with exceptions
but must be absolutely necessary. Clearly, therefore, no experience can
give occasion for inferring even the possibility of such apodeictic laws.
For with what right could we bring into unlimited respect as a universal
precept for every rational nature what is perhaps valid only under the
contingent conditions of humanity? And how could laws for the determination of our will be regarded as laws for the determination of a rational being in general and of ourselves only insofar as we are rational beings, if these laws were merely empirical and did not have their source
completely a priori in pure, but practical, reason?

Moreover, worse service cannot be rendered morality than that an attempt be made to derive it from examples. For every example of morality
presented to me must itself first be judged according to principles of
morality in order to see whether it is fit to serve as an original example,
i.e., as a model. But in no way can it authoritatively furnish the concept

of morality. Even the Holy One of the gospel must first be compared with our ideal of moral perfection before he is recognized as such. Even he says of himself, "Why do you call me (whom you see) good? None is good (the archetype of the good) except God only (whom you do not see)." But whence have we the concept of God as the highest good? Solely from the idea of moral perfection, which reason frames a priori and connects inseparably with the concept of a free will. Imitation has no place at all in moral matters. And examples serve only for encouragement, i.e., they put beyond doubt the feasibility of what the law commands and they make visible what the practical rule expresses more generally. But examples can never justify us in setting aside their true original, which lies in reason, and letting ourselves be guided by them.

If there is then no genuine supreme principle of morality which does not rest on pure reason alone, independent of all experience, I think it is unnecessary even to ask whether it is a good thing to exhibit these concepts generally (*in abstracto*), which, along with the principles that belong to them, hold a priori, so far as the knowledge involved is to be distinguished from ordinary knowledge and is to be called philosophical. But in our times it may well be necessary to do so. For if one were to take a vote as to whether pure rational knowledge separated from everything empirical, i.e., metaphysics of morals, or whether popular practical philosophy is to be preferred, one can easily guess which side would be preponderant.

This descent to popular thought is certainly very commendable once the ascent to the principles of pure reason has occurred and has been satisfactorily accomplished. That would mean that the doctrine of morals has first been grounded on metaphysics and that subsequently acceptance for morals has been won by giving it a popular character after it has been firmly established. But it is quite absurd to try for popularity in the first inquiry, upon which depends the total correctness of the principles. Not only can such a procedure never lay claim to the very rare merit of a true philosophical popularity, inasmuch as there is really no art involved at all in being generally intelligible if one thereby renounces all basic insight, but such a procedure turns out a disgusting mishmash of patchwork observations and half-reasoned principles in which shallowpates revel because all this is something quite useful for the chitchat of everyday life. Persons of insight, on the other hand, feel confused by all this and turn their eyes away with a dissatisfaction which they nevertheless cannot cure. Yet philosophers, who quite see through the delusion, get little hearing when they summon people for a time from this pretended popularity in order that they may be rightfully popular only after they have attained definite insight.

One need only look at the attempts to deal with morality in the way favored by popular taste. What he will find in an amazing mixture is at one time the particular constitution of human nature (but along with this also the idea of a rational nature in general), at another time perfection, at another happiness; here moral feeling, and there the fear of God; something of this, and also something of that. But the thought never occurs to ask whether the principles of morality are to be sought at all in the knowledge of human nature (which can be had only from experience). Nor does the thought occur that if these principles are not to be sought here but to be found, rather, completely a priori and free from everything empirical in pure rational concepts only, and are to be found nowhere else even to the slightest extent—then there had better be adopted the plan of undertaking this investigation as a separate inquiry, i.e., as pure practical philosophy or (if one may use a name so much decried) as a metaphysics[1] of morals. It is better to bring this investigation to full completeness entirely by itself and to bid the public, which demands popularity, to await the outcome of this undertaking.

But such a completely isolated metaphysics of morals, not mixed with any anthropology, theology, physics, or hyperphysics, and still less with occult qualities (which might be called hypophysical), is not only an indispensable substratum of all theoretical and precisely defined knowledge of duties, but is at the same time a desideratum of the highest importance for the actual fulfillment of their precepts. For the pure thought of duty and of the moral law generally, unmixed with any extraneous addition of empirical inducements, has by the way of reason alone (which first becomes aware hereby that it can of itself be practical) an influence on 411 the human heart so much more powerful than all other incentives[2] which may be derived from the empirical field that reason in the consciousness of its dignity despises such incentives and is able gradually to become their master. On the other hand, a mixed moral philosophy, compounded both of incentives drawn from feelings and inclinations and at the same time of rational concepts, must make the mind waver between motives that cannot be brought under any principle and that can only by accident lead to the good but often can also lead to the bad.

It is clear from the foregoing that all moral concepts have their seat and origin completely a priori in reason, and indeed in the most ordinary

1. Pure philosophy of morals (metaphysics) may be distinguished from the applied (viz., applied to human nature) just as pure mathematics is distinguished from applied mathematics and pure logic from applied logic. By this designation one is also immediately reminded that moral principles are not grounded on the peculiarities of human nature but must subsist a priori of themselves, and that from such principles practical rules must be derivable for every rational nature, and accordingly for human nature.

2. I have a letter from the late excellent Sulzer [Johann Georg Sulzer (1720–1779), an important Berlin savant, who translated Hume's *Inquiry Concerning the Principles of Morals* into German in 1755] in which he asks me why it is that moral instruction accomplishes so little, even though it contains so much that is convincing to reason. My answer was delayed so that I might make it complete. But it is just that the teachers themselves have not purified their concepts: since they try to do too well by looking everywhere for motives for being morally good, they spoil the medicine by trying to make it really strong. For the most ordinary observation shows that when a righteous act is represented as being done with a steadfast soul and sundered from all view to any advantage in this or another world, and even under the greatest temptations of need or allurement, it far surpasses and eclipses any similar action that was in the least affected by any extraneous incentive; it elevates the soul and inspires the wish to be able to act in this way. Even moderately young children feel this impression, and duties should never be represented to them in any other way.

human reason just as much as in the most highly speculative. They cannot be abstracted from any empirical, and hence merely contingent, cognition. In this purity of their origin lies their very worthiness to serve us as supreme practical principles; and to the extent that something empirical is added to them, just so much is taken away from their genuine influence and from the absolute worth of the corresponding actions. Moreover, it is not only a requirement of the greatest necessity from a theoretical point of view, when it is a question of speculation, but also of the greatest practical importance, to draw these concepts and laws from pure reason, to present them pure and unmixed, and indeed to determine the extent of this entire practical and pure rational cognition, i.e., to determine the whole faculty of pure practical reason. The principles should not be made 412 to depend on the particular nature of human reason, as speculative philosophy may permit and even sometimes finds necessary; but, rather, the principles should be derived from the universal concept of a rational being in general, since moral laws should hold for every rational being as such. In this way all morals, which require anthropology in order to be applied to humans, must be entirely expounded at first independently of anthropology as pure philosophy, i.e., as metaphysics (which can easily be done in such distinct kinds of knowledge). One knows quite well that unless one is in possession of such a metaphysics, then the attempt is futile, I shall not say to determine exactly for speculative judgment the moral element of duty in all that accords with duty, but that the attempt is impossible, even in ordinary and practical usage, especially in that of moral instruction, to ground morals on their genuine principles and thereby to produce pure moral dispositions and engraft them on men's minds for the promotion of the highest good in the world.

In this study we must advance by natural stages not merely from ordinary moral judgment (which is here ever so worthy of respect) to philosophical judgment, as has already been done, but also from popular philosophy, which goes no further than it can get by groping about with the help of examples, to metaphysics (which does not permit itself to be held back any longer by what is empirical, and which, inasmuch as it must survey the whole extent of rational knowledge of this kind, goes right up to ideas, where examples themselves fail us). In order to make such an advance, we must follow and clearly present the practical faculty of reason from its universal rules of determination to the point where the concept of duty springs from it.

Everything in nature works according to laws. Only a rational being has the power to act according to his conception of laws, i.e., according to principles, and thereby has he a will. Since the derivation of actions from laws requires reason, the will is nothing but practical reason. If reason infallibly determines the will, then in the case of such a being actions which are recognized to be objectively necessary are also subjectively necessary, i.e., the will is a faculty of choosing only that which reason, independently of inclination, recognizes as being practically necessary, i.e., as good. But if reason of itself does not sufficiently determine the will, and if the

413   will submits also to subjective conditions (certain incentives) which do not always agree with objective conditions; in a word, if the will does not in itself completely accord with reason (as is actually the case with men), then actions which are recognized as objectively necessary are subjectively contingent, and the determination of such a will according to objective laws is necessitation. That is to say that the relation of objective laws to a will not thoroughly good is represented as the determination of the will of a rational being by principles of reason which the will does not necessarily follow because of its own nature.

The representation of an objective principle insofar as it necessitates the will is called a command (of reason), and the formula of the command is called an imperative.

All imperatives are expressed by an *ought* and thereby indicate the relation of an objective law of reason to a will that is not necessarily determined by this law because of its subjective constitution (the relation of necessitation). Imperatives say that something would be good to do or to refrain from doing, but they say it to a will that does not always therefore do something simply because it has been represented to the will as something good to do. That is practically good which determines the will by means of representations of reason and hence not by subjective causes, but objectively, i.e., on grounds valid for every rational being as such. It is distinguished from the pleasant as that which influences the will only by means of sensation from merely subjective causes, which hold only for this or that person's senses but do not hold as a principle of reason valid for everyone.[3]

414   A perfectly good will would thus be quite as much subject to objective laws (of the good), but could not be conceived as thereby necessitated to act in conformity with law, inasmuch as it can of itself, according to its subjective constitution, be determined only by the representation of the good. Therefore no imperatives hold for the divine will, and in general for a holy will; the *ought* is here out of place, because the *would* is already of itself necessarily in agreement with the law. Consequently, imperatives are only formulas for expressing the relation of objective laws of willing in general to the subjective imperfection of the will of this or that rational being, e.g., the human will.

3. The dependence of the faculty of desire on sensations is called inclination, which accordingly always indicates a need. The dependence of a contingently determinable will on principles of reason, however, is called interest. Therefore an interest is found only in a dependent will which is not of itself always in accord with reason; in the divine will no interest can be thought. But even the human will can take an interest in something without thereby acting from interest. The former signifies practical interest in the action, while the latter signifies pathological interest in the object of the action. The former indicates only dependence of the will on principles of reason by itself, while the latter indicates the will's dependence on principles of reason for the sake of inclination, i.e., reason merely gives the practical rule for meeting the need of inclination. In the former case the action interests me, while in the latter case what interests me is the object of the action (so far as this object is pleasant for me). In the First Section we have seen that in the case of an action done from duty regard must be given not to the interest in the object, but only to interest in the action itself and in its rational principle (viz., the law).

Now all imperatives command either hypothetically or categorically. The former represent the practical necessity of a possible action as a means for attaining something else that one wants (or may possibly want). The categorical imperative would be one which represented an action as objectively necessary in itself, without reference to another end.

Every practical law represents a possible action as good and hence as necessary for a subject who is practically determinable by reason; therefore all imperatives are formulas for determining an action which is necessary according to the principle of a will that is good in some way. Now if the action would be good merely as a means to something else, so is the imperative hypothetical. But if the action is represented as good in itself, and hence as necessary in a will which of itself conforms to reason as the principle of the will, then the imperative is categorical.

An imperative thus says what action possible by me would be good, and it presents the practical rule in relation to a will which does not forthwith perform an action simply because it is good, partly because the subject does not always know that the action is good and partly because (even if he does know it is good) his maxims might yet be opposed to the objective principles of practical reason.

A hypothetical imperative thus says only that an action is good for some purpose, either possible or actual. In the first case it is a problematic practical principle; in the second case an assertoric one. A categorical imperative, which declares an action to be of itself objectively necessary without reference to any purpose, i.e., without any other end, holds as an apodeictic practical principle.

Whatever is possible only through the powers of some rational being can be thought of as a possible purpose of some will. Consequently, there are in fact infinitely many principles of action insofar as they are represented as necessary for attaining a possible purpose achievable by them. All sciences have a practical part consisting of problems saying that some end is possible for us and of imperatives telling us how it can be attained. These can, therefore, be called in general imperatives of skill. Here there is no question at all whether the end is reasonable and good, but there is only a question as to what must be done to attain it. The prescriptions needed by a doctor in order to make his patient thoroughly healthy and by a poisoner in order to make sure of killing his victim are of equal value so far as each serves to bring about its purpose perfectly. Since there cannot be known in early youth what ends may be presented to us in the course of life, parents especially seek to have their children learn many different kinds of things, and they provide for skill in the use of means to all sorts of arbitrary ends, among which they cannot determine whether any one of them could in the future become an actual purpose for their ward, though there is always the possibility that he might adopt it. Their concern is so great that they commonly neglect to form and correct their children's judgment regarding the worth of things which might be chosen as ends.

415

There is, however, one end that can be presupposed as actual for all rational beings (so far as they are dependent beings to whom imperatives apply); and thus there is one purpose which they not merely can have but which can certainly be assumed to be such that they all do have by a natural necessity, and this is happiness. A hypothetical imperative which represents the practical necessity of an action as means for the promotion of happiness is assertoric. It may be expounded not simply as necessary to an uncertain, merely possible purpose, but as necessary to a purpose which can be presupposed a priori and with certainty as being present in everyone because it belongs to his essence. Now skill in the choice of means to one's own greatest well-being can be called prudence[4] in the narrowest sense. And thus the imperative that refers to the choice of means to one's own happiness, i.e., the precept of prudence, still remains hypothetical; the action is commanded not absolutely but only as a means to a further purpose.

Finally, there is one imperative which immediately commands a certain conduct without having as its condition any other purpose to be attained by it. This imperative is categorical. It is not concerned with the matter of the action and its intended result, but rather with the form of the action and the principle from which it follows; what is essentially good in the action consists in the mental disposition, let the consequences be what they may. This imperative may be called that of morality.

Willing according to these three kinds of principles is also clearly distinguished by dissimilarity in the necessitation of the will. To make this dissimilarity clear I think that they are most suitably named in their order when they are said to be either *rules of skill, counsels of prudence,* or *commands (laws) of morality.* For law alone involves the concept of a necessity that is unconditioned and indeed objective and hence universally valid, and commands are laws which must be obeyed, i.e., must be followed even in opposition to inclination. Counsel does indeed involve necessity, but involves such necessity as is valid only under a subjectively contingent condition, viz., whether this or that man counts this or that as belonging to his happiness. On the other hand, the categorical imperative is limited by no condition, and can quite properly be called a command since it is absolutely, though practically, necessary. The first kind of imperatives might also be called technical (belonging to art), the second kind pragmatic[5]

416

417

---

4. The word "prudence" is used in a double sense: firstly, it can mean worldly wisdom, and, secondly, private wisdom. The former is the skill of someone in influencing others so as to use them for his own purposes. The latter is the sagacity to combine all these purposes for his own lasting advantage. The value of the former is properly reduced to the latter, and it might better be said of one who is prudent in the former sense but not in the latter that he is clever and cunning, but on the whole imprudent.

5. It seems to me that the proper meaning of the word "pragmatic" could be defined most accurately in this way. For those sanctions are called pragmatic which properly flow not from the law of states as necessary enactments but from provision for the general welfare. A history is pragmatically written when it teaches prudence, i.e., instructs the world how it can provide for its interests better than, or at least as well as, has been done in former times.

(belonging to welfare), the third kind moral (belonging to free conduct as such, i.e., to morals).

The question now arises: how are all of these imperatives possible?[6] This question does not seek to know how the fulfillment of the action commanded by the imperative can be conceived, but merely how the necessitation of the will expressed by the imperative in setting a task can be conceived. How an imperative of skill is possible requires no special discussion. Whoever wills the end, wills (so far as reason has decisive influence on his actions) also the means that are indispensably necessary to his actions and that lie in his power. This proposition, as far as willing is concerned, is analytic. For in willing an object as my effect there is already thought the causality of myself as an acting cause, i.e., the use of means. The imperative derives the concept of actions necessary to this end from the concept of willing this end. (Synthetic propositions are indeed required for determining the means to a proposed end; but such propositions are concerned not with the ground, i.e., the act of the will, but only with the way to realize the object of the will.) Mathematics teaches by nothing but synthetic propositions that in order to bisect a line according to a sure principle I must from each of its extremities draw arcs such that they intersect. But when I know that the proposed result can come about only by means of such an action, then the proposition (if I fully will the effect, then I also will the action required for it) is analytic. For it is one and the same thing to conceive of something as an effect that is possible in a certain way through me and to conceive of myself as acting in the same way with regard to the aforesaid effect.

If it were only as easy to give a determinate concept of happiness, then the imperatives of prudence would exactly correspond to those of skill and would be likewise analytic. For there could be said in this case just as   418 in the former that whoever wills the end also wills (necessarily according to reason) the sole means thereto which are in his power. But, unfortunately, the concept of happiness is such an indeterminate one that even though everyone wishes to attain happiness, yet he can never say definitely and consistently what it is that he really wishes and wills. The reason for this is that all the elements belonging to the concept of happiness are unexceptionally empirical, i.e., they must be borrowed from experience, while for the idea of happiness there is required an absolute whole, a maximum of well-being in my present and in every future condition. Now it is impossible for the most insightful and at the same time most powerful, but nonetheless finite, being to frame here a determinate concept of what it is that he really wills. Does he want riches? How much anxiety, envy, and intrigue might he not thereby bring down upon his own head! Or knowledge and insight? Perhaps these might only give him an eye that much sharper for revealing that much more dreadfully evils which are at present hidden but are yet unavoidable, or such an eye

---

6. [That is, why should one let his actions be determined at various times by one or the other of these three kinds of imperatives?]

might burden him with still further needs for the desires which already concern him enough. Or long life? Who guarantees that it would not be a long misery? Or health at least? How often has infirmity of the body kept one from excesses into which perfect health would have allowed him to fall, and so on? In brief, he is not able on any principle to determine with complete certainty what will make him truly happy, because to do so would require omniscience. Therefore, one cannot act according to determinate principles in order to be happy, but only according to empirical counsels, e.g., of diet, frugality, politeness, reserve, etc., which are shown by experience to contribute on the average the most to well-being. There follows from this that imperatives of prudence, strictly speaking, cannot command at all, i.e., present actions objectively as practically necessary. They are to be taken as counsels (*consilia*) rather than as commands (*praecepta*) of reason. The problem of determining certainly and universally what action will promote the happiness of a rational being is completely insoluble. Therefore, regarding such action no imperative that in the strictest sense could command what is to be done to make one happy is possible, inasmuch as happiness is not an ideal of
419 reason but of imagination. Such an ideal rests merely on empirical grounds; in vain can there be expected that such grounds should determine an action whereby the totality of an infinite series of consequences could be attained. This imperative of prudence would, nevertheless, be an analytic practical proposition if one assumes that the means to happiness could with certainty be assigned; for it differs from the imperative of skill only in that for it the end is given while for the latter the end is merely possible. Since both, however, command only the means to what is assumed to be willed as an end, the imperative commanding him who wills the end to will likewise the means thereto is in both cases analytic. Hence there is also no difficulty regarding the possibility of an imperative of prudence.

On the other hand, the question as to how the imperative of morality is possible is undoubtedly the only one requiring a solution. For it is not at all hypothetical; and hence the objective necessity which it presents cannot be based on any presupposition, as was the case with the hypothetical imperatives. Only there must never here be forgotten that no example can show, i.e., empirically, whether there is any such imperative at all. Rather, care must be taken lest all imperatives which are seemingly categorical may nevertheless be covertly hypothetical. For instance, when it is said that you should not make a false promise, the assumption is that the necessity of this avoidance is no mere advice for escaping some other evil, so that it might be said that you should not make a false promise lest you ruin your credit when the falsity comes to light. But when it is asserted that an action of this kind must be regarded as bad in itself, then the imperative of prohibition is therefore categorical. Nevertheless, it cannot with certainty be shown by means of an example that the will is here determined solely by the law without any other incentive, even though such may seem to be the case. For it is always possible that secretly there is fear of disgrace and perhaps also obscure dread of other dangers; such fear and dread may have influenced the will. Who can prove by experience that a cause is not present? Experience only shows that a cause is not perceived. But in such a case the so-called moral imperative, which as such appears to be categorical and unconditioned, would actually be only a pragmatic precept which makes us pay attention to our own advantage and merely teaches us to take such advantage into consideration.

We shall, therefore, have to investigate the possibility of a categorical imperative entirely a priori, inasmuch as we do not here have the advantage of having its reality given in experience and consequently of thus being obligated merely to explain its possibility rather than to establish it. In the meantime so much can be seen for now: the categorical imperative alone purports to be a practical law, while all the others may be called principles of the will but not laws. The reason for this is that whatever is necessary merely in order to attain some arbitrary purpose can be regarded as in itself contingent, and the precept can always be ignored once the purpose is abandoned. Contrariwise, an unconditioned command does not leave the will free to choose the opposite at its own liking. Consequently, only such a command carries with it that necessity which is demanded from a law.

420

Secondly, in the case of this categorical imperative, or law of morality, the reason for the difficulty (of discerning its possibility) is quite serious. The categorical imperative is an a priori synthetic practical proposition;[7] and since discerning the possibility of propositions of this sort involves so much difficulty in theoretic knowledge, there may readily be gathered that there will be no less difficulty in practical knowledge.

In solving this problem, we want first to inquire whether perhaps the mere concept of a categorical imperative may not also supply us with the formula containing the proposition that can alone be a categorical imperative. For even when we know the purport of such an absolute command, the question as to how it is possible will still require a special and difficult effort, which we postpone to the last section.[8]

If I think of a hypothetical imperative in general, I do not know beforehand what it will contain until its condition is given. But if I think of a categorical imperative, I know immediately what it contains. For since, besides the law, the imperative contains only the necessity that the

---

7. I connect a priori, and therefore necessarily, the act with the will without presupposing any condition taken from some inclination (though I make such a connection only objectively, i.e., under the idea of a reason having full power over all subjective motives). Hence this is a practical proposition which does not analytically derive the willing of an action from some other willing already presupposed (for we possess no such perfect will) but which connects the willing of an action immediately with the concept of the will of a rational being as something which is not contained in this concept.

8. [See below Ak. 446–63.]

421 maxim[9] should accord with this law, while the law contains no condition to restrict it, there remains nothing but the universality of a law as such with which the maxim of the action should conform. This conformity alone is properly what is represented as necessary by the imperative.

Hence there is only one categorical imperative and it is this: Act only according to that maxim whereby you can at the same time will that it should become a universal law.[10]

Now if all imperatives of duty can be derived from this one imperative as their principle, then there can at least be shown what is understood by the concept of duty and what it means, even though there is left undecided whether what is called duty may not be an empty concept.

The universality of law according to which effects are produced constitutes what is properly called nature in the most general sense (as to form), i.e., the existence of things as far as determined by universal laws. Accordingly, the universal imperative of duty may be expressed thus: Act as if the maxim of your action were to become through your will a universal law of nature.[11]

We shall now enumerate some duties, following the usual division of them into duties to ourselves and to others and into perfect and imperfect duties.[12]

1. A man reduced to despair by a series of misfortunes feels sick of life
422 but is still so far in possession of his reason that he can ask himself whether taking his own life would not be contrary to his duty to himself.[13] Now he asks whether the maxim of his action could become a universal law of nature. But his maxim is this: from self-love I make as my principle to shorten my life when its continued duration threatens more evil than it promises satisfaction. There only remains the question as to whether this

9. A maxim is the subjective principle of acting and must be distinguished from the objective principle, viz., the practical law. A maxim contains the practical rule which reason determines in accordance with the conditions of the subject (often his ignorance or his inclinations) and is thus the principle according to which the subject does act. But the law is the objective principle valid for every rational being, and it is the principle according to which he ought to act, i.e., an imperative.

10. [This formulation of the categorical imperative is often referred to as the formula of universal law.]

11. [This is often called the formula of the law of nature.]

12. There should be noted here that I reserve the division of duties for a future *Metaphysics of Morals* [in Part II of the *Metaphysics of Morals*, entitled *The Metaphysical Principles of Virtue*, Ak. 417–474]. The division presented here stands as merely an arbitrary one (in order to arrange my examples). For the rest, I understand here by a perfect duty one which permits no exception in the interest of inclination. Accordingly, I have perfect duties which are external [to others], while other ones are internal [to oneself]. This classification runs contrary to the accepted usage of the schools, but I do not intend to justify it here, since there is no difference for my purpose whether this classification is accepted or not.

13. [Not committing suicide is an example of a perfect duty to oneself. See *Metaphysical Principles of Virtue*, Ak. 422–24.]

principle of self-love can become a universal law of nature. One sees at once a contradiction in a system of nature whose law would destroy life by means of the very same feeling that acts so as to stimulate the furtherance of life, and hence there could be no existence as a system of nature. Therefore, such a maxim cannot possibly hold as a universal law of nature and is, consequently, wholly opposed to the supreme principle of all duty.

2. Another man in need finds himself forced to borrow money. He knows well that he won't be able to repay it, but he sees also that he will not get any loan unless he firmly promises to repay it within a fixed time. He wants to make such a promise, but he still has conscience enough to ask himself whether it is not permissible and is contrary to duty to get out of difficulty in this way. Suppose, however, that he decides to do so. The maxim of his action would then be expressed as follows: when I believe myself to be in need of money, I will borrow money and promise to pay it back, although I know that I can never do so. Now this principle of self-love or personal advantage may perhaps be quite compatible with one's entire future welfare, but the question is now whether it is right.[14] I then transform the requirement of self-love into a universal law and put the question thus: how would things stand if my maxim were to become a universal law? He then sees at once that such a maxim could never hold as a universal law of nature and be consistent with itself, but must necessarily be self-contradictory. For the universality of a law which says that anyone believing himself to be in difficulty could promise whatever he pleases with the intention of not keeping it would make promising itself and the end to be attained thereby quite impossible, inasmuch as no one would believe what was promised him but would merely laugh at all such utterances as being vain pretenses.

3. A third finds in himself a talent whose cultivation could make him a man useful in many respects. But he finds himself in comfortable cir- 423 cumstances and prefers to indulge in pleasure rather than to bother himself about broadening and improving his fortunate natural aptitudes. But he asks himself further whether his maxim of neglecting his natural gifts, besides agreeing of itself with his propensity to indulgence, might agree also with what is called duty.[15] He then sees that a system of nature could indeed always subsist according to such a universal law, even though every man (like South Sea Islanders) should let his talents rust and resolve to devote his life entirely to idleness, indulgence, propagation, and, in a word, to enjoyment. But he cannot possibly will that this should become a universal law of nature or be implanted in us as such a law by a natural instinct. For as a rational being he necessarily wills that all his faculties should be developed, inasmuch as they are given him for all sorts of possible purposes.

14. [Keeping promises is an example of a perfect duty to others. See *ibid.*, Ak. 423–31.]

15. [Cultivating one's talents is an example of an imperfect duty to oneself. See *ibid.*, Ak. 444–46.]

4. A fourth man finds things going well for himself but sees others (whom he could help) struggling with great hardships; and he thinks: what does it matter to me? Let everybody be as happy as Heaven wills or as he can make himself; I shall take nothing from him nor even envy him; but I have no desire to contribute anything to his well-being or to his assistance when in need. If such a way of thinking were to become a universal law of nature, the human race admittedly could very well subsist and doubtless could subsist even better than when everyone prates about sympathy and benevolence and even on occasion exerts himself to practice them but, on the other hand, also cheats when he can, betrays the rights of man, or otherwise violates them. But even though it is possible that a universal law of nature could subsist in accordance with that maxim, still it is impossible to will that such a principle should hold everywhere as a law of nature.[16] For a will which resolved in this way would contradict itself, inasmuch as cases might often arise in which one would have need of the love and sympathy of others and in which he would deprive himself, by such a law of nature springing from his own will, of all hope of the aid he wants for himself.

424 These are some of the many actual duties, or at least what are taken to be such, whose derivation from the single principle cited above is clear. We must be able to will that a maxim of our action become a universal law; this is the canon for morally estimating any of our actions. Some actions are so constituted that their maxims cannot without contradiction even be thought as a universal law of nature, much less be willed as what should become one. In the case of others this internal impossibility is indeed not found, but there is still no possibility of willing that their maxim should be raised to the universality of a law of nature, because such a will would contradict itself. There is no difficulty in seeing that the former kind of action conflicts with strict or narrow [perfect] (irremissible) duty, while the second kind conflicts only with broad [imperfect] (meritorious) duty.[17] By means of these examples there has thus been fully set forth how all duties depend as regards the kind of obligation (not the object of their action) upon the one principle.

If we now attend to ourselves in any transgression of a duty, we find that we actually do not will that our maxim should become a universal law—because this is impossible for us—but rather that the opposite of this maxim should remain a law universally.[18] We only take the liberty of making an exception to the law for ourselves (or just for this one time) to

---

16. [Benefiting others is an example of an imperfect duty to others. See *ibid.*, Ak. 452–54.]

17. [Compare *ibid.*, Ak. 390–94, 410–11, 421–51.]

18. [This is to say, for example, that when you tell a lie, you do so on the condition that others are truthful and believe that what you are saying is true, because otherwise your lie will never work to get you what you want. When you tell a lie, you simply take exception to the general rule that says everyone should always tell the truth.]

the advantage of our inclination. Consequently, if we weighed up everything from one and the same standpoint, namely, that of reason, we would find a contradiction in our own will, viz., that a certain principle be objectively necessary as a universal law and yet subjectively not hold universally but should admit of exceptions. But since we at one moment regard our action from the standpoint of a will wholly in accord with reason and then at another moment regard the very same action from the standpoint of a will affected by inclination, there is really no contradiction here. Rather, there is an opposition (*antagonismus*) of inclination to the precept of reason, whereby the universality (*universalitas*) of the principle is changed into a mere generality (*generalitas*) so that the practical principle of reason may meet the maxim halfway. Although this procedure cannot be justified in our own impartial judgment, yet it does show that we actually acknowledge the validity of the categorical imperative and (with all respect for it) merely allow ourselves a few exceptions which, as they seem to us, are unimportant and forced upon us.

We have thus at least shown that if duty is a concept which is to have   425
significance and real legislative authority for our actions, then such duty can be expressed only in categorical imperatives but not at all in hypothetical ones. We have also—and this is already a great deal—exhibited clearly and definitely for every application what is the content of the categorical imperative, which must contain the principle of all duty (if there is such a thing at all). But we have not yet advanced far enough to prove a priori that there actually is an imperative of this kind, that there is a practical law which of itself commands absolutely and without any incentives, and that following this law is duty.

In order to attain this proof there is the utmost importance in being warned that we must not take it into our mind to derive the reality of this principle from the special characteristics of human nature. For duty has to be a practical, unconditioned necessity of action; hence it must hold for all rational beings (to whom alone an imperative is at all applicable) and for this reason only can it also be a law for all human wills. On the other hand, whatever is derived from the special natural condition of humanity, from certain feelings and propensities, or even, if such were possible, from some special tendency peculiar to human reason and not holding necessarily for the will of every rational being—all of this can indeed yield a maxim valid for us, but not a law. This is to say that such can yield a subjective principle according to which we might act if we happen to have the propensity and inclination, but cannot yield an objective principle according to which we would be directed to act even though our every propensity, inclination, and natural tendency were opposed to it. In fact, the sublimity and inner worth of the command are so much the more evident in a duty, the fewer subjective causes there are for it and the more they oppose it; such causes do not in the least weaken the necessitation exerted by the law or take away anything from its validity.

Here philosophy is seen in fact to be put in a precarious position, which should be firm even though there is neither in heaven nor on earth anything upon which it depends or is based. Here philosophy must show its purity as author of its laws, and not as the herald of such laws as are whispered to it by an implanted sense or by who knows what tutelary nature. Such laws may be better than nothing at all, but they can never

426   give us principles dictated by reason. These principles must have an origin that is completely a priori and must at the same time derive from such origin their authority to command. They expect nothing from the inclination of men but, rather, expect everything from the supremacy of the law and from the respect owed to the law. Without the latter expectation, these principles condemn man to self-contempt and inward abhorrence.

Hence everything empirical is not only quite unsuitable as a contribution to the principle of morality, but is even highly detrimental to the purity of morals. For the proper and inestimable worth of an absolutely good will consists precisely in the fact that the principle of action is free of all influences from contingent grounds, which only experience can furnish. This lax or even mean way of thinking which seeks its principle among empirical motives and laws cannot too much or too often be warned against, for human reason in its weariness is glad to rest upon this pillow. In a dream of sweet illusions (in which not Juno but a cloud is embraced) there is substituted for morality some bastard patched up from limbs of quite varied ancestry and looking like anything one wants to see in it but not looking like virtue to him who has once beheld her in her true form.[19]

Therefore, the question is this: is it a necessary law for all rational beings always to judge their actions according to such maxims as they can themselves will that such should serve as universal laws? If there is such a law, then it must already be connected (completely a priori) with the concept of the will of a rational being in general. But in order to discover this connection we must, however reluctantly, take a step into metaphysics, although into a region of it different from speculative philosophy, i.e., we must enter the metaphysics of morals. In practical philosophy the concern is

427   not with accepting grounds for what happens but with accepting laws of what ought to happen, even though it never does happen—that is, the concern is with objectively practical laws. Here there is no need to inquire into the grounds as to why something pleases or displeases, how the pleasure of mere sensation differs from taste, and whether taste differs from a general satisfaction of reason, upon what does the feeling of pleasure and displeasure rest, and how from this feeling desires and inclinations arise, and how, finally, from these there arise maxims through the cooperation

19. To behold virtue in her proper form is nothing other than to present morality stripped of all admixture of what is sensuous and of every spurious adornment of reward or self-love. How much she then eclipses all else that appears attractive to the inclinations can be easily seen by everyone with the least effort of his reason, if it be not entirely ruined for all abstraction.

of reason. All of this belongs to an empirical psychology, which would constitute the second part of the doctrine of nature, if this doctrine is regarded as the philosophy of nature insofar as this philosophy is grounded on empirical laws. But here the concern is with objectively practical laws, and hence with the relation of a will to itself insofar as it is determined solely by reason. In this case everything related to what is empirical falls away of itself, because if reason entirely by itself determines conduct (and the possibility of such determination we now wish to investigate), then reason must necessarily do so a priori.

The will is thought of as a faculty of determining itself to action in accordance with the representation of certain laws, and such a faculty can be found only in rational beings. Now what serves the will as the objective ground of its self-determination is an end; and if this end is given by reason alone, then it must be equally valid for all rational beings. On the other hand, what contains merely the ground of the possibility of the action, whose effect is an end, is called the means. The subjective ground of desire is the incentive; the objective ground of volition is the motive. Hence there arises the distinction between subjective ends, which rest on incentives, and objective ends, which depend on motives valid for every rational being. Practical principles are formal when they abstract from all subjective ends; they are material, however, when they are founded upon subjective ends, and hence upon certain incentives. The ends which a rational being arbitrarily proposes to himself as effects of this action (material ends) are all merely relative, for only their relation to a specially constituted faculty of desire in the subject gives them their worth. Consequently, such worth cannot provide any universal principles, which are valid and necessary for all rational beings and, furthermore, are valid for 428 every volition, i.e., cannot provide any practical laws. Therefore, all such relative ends can be grounds only for hypothetical imperatives.

But let us suppose that there were something whose existence has in itself an absolute worth, something which as an end in itself could be a ground of determinate laws. In it, and in it alone, would there be the ground of a possible categorical imperative, i.e., of a practical law.

Now I say that man, and in general every rational being, exists as an end in himself and not merely as a means to be arbitrarily used by this or that will. He must in all his actions, whether directed to himself or to other rational beings, always be regarded at the same time as an end. All the objects of inclinations have only a conditioned value; for if there were not these inclinations and the needs founded on them, then their object would be without value. But the inclinations themselves, being sources of needs, are so far from having an absolute value such as to render them desirable for their own sake that the universal wish of every rational being must be, rather, to be wholly free from them. Accordingly, the value of any object obtainable by our action is always conditioned. Beings whose existence depends not on our will but on nature have, nevertheless, if they are not rational beings, only a relative value as means and are therefore called things. On the other hand, rational beings are called persons inasmuch as their nature already marks them out as ends in themselves, i.e., as something which is not to be used merely as means and hence there is imposed thereby a limit on all arbitrary use of such beings, which are thus objects of respect. Persons are, therefore, not merely subjective ends, whose existence as an effect of our actions has a value for us; but such beings are objective ends, i.e., exist as ends in themselves. Such an end is one for which there can be substituted no other end to which such beings should serve merely as means, for otherwise nothing at all of absolute value would be found anywhere. But if all value were conditioned and hence contingent, then no supreme practical principle could be found for reason at all.

If then there is to be a supreme practical principle and, as far as the human will is concerned, a categorical imperative, then it must be such that from the conception of what is necessarily an end for everyone because this end is an end in itself it constitutes an objective principle of

429 the will and can hence serve as a practical law. The ground of such a principle is this: rational nature exists as an end in itself. In this way man necessarily thinks of his own existence; thus far is it a subjective principle of human actions. But in this way also does every other rational being think of his existence on the same rational ground that holds also for me;[20] hence it is at the same time an objective principle, from which, as a supreme practical ground, all laws of the will must be able to be derived. The practical imperative will therefore be the following: Act in such a way that you treat humanity, whether in your own person or in the person of another, always at the same time as an end and never simply as a means.[21] We now want to see whether this can be carried out in practice.

Let us keep to our previous examples.[22]

First, as regards the concept of necessary duty to oneself, the man who contemplates suicide will ask himself whether his action can be consistent with the idea of humanity as an end in itself. If he destroys himself in order to escape from a difficult situation, then he is making use of his person merely as a means so as to maintain a tolerable condition till the end of his life. Man, however, is not a thing and hence is not something to be used merely as a means; he must in all his actions always be regarded as an end in himself. Therefore, I cannot dispose of man in my own person by mutilating, damaging, or killing him. (A more exact determination of this principle so as to avoid all misunderstanding, e.g., regarding the amputation of limbs in order to save oneself, or the exposure of one's life to

20. This proposition I here put forward as a postulate. The grounds for it will be found in the last section. [See below Ak. 446–63.]

21. [This oft-quoted version of the categorical imperative is usually referred to as the formula of the end in itself.]

22. [See above Ak. 422–23.]

danger in order to save it, and so on, must here be omitted; such questions belong to morals proper.)

Second, as concerns necessary or strict duty to others, the man who intends to make a false promise will immediately see that he intends to make use of another man merely as a means to an end which the latter does not likewise hold. For the man whom I want to use for my own purposes by such a promise cannot possibly concur with my way of acting toward him 430 and hence cannot himself hold the end of this action. This conflict with the principle of duty to others becomes even clearer when instances of attacks on the freedom and property of others are considered. For then it becomes clear that a transgressor of the rights of men intends to make use of the persons of others merely as a means, without taking into consideration that, as rational beings, they should always be esteemed at the same time as ends, i.e., be esteemed only as beings who must themselves be able to hold the very same action as an end.[23]

Third, with regard to contingent (meritorious) duty to oneself, it is not enough that the action does not conflict with humanity in our own person as an end in itself; the action must also harmonize with this end. Now there are in humanity capacities for greater perfection which belong to the end that nature has in view as regards humanity in our own person. To neglect these capacities might perhaps be consistent with the maintenance of humanity as an end in itself, but would not be consistent with the advancement of this end.

Fourth, concerning meritorious duty to others, the natural end that all men have is their own happiness. Now humanity might indeed subsist if nobody contributed anything to the happiness of others, provided he did not intentionally impair their happiness. But this, after all, would harmonize only negatively and not positively with humanity as an end in itself, if everyone does not also strive, as much as he can, to further the ends of others. For the ends of any subject who is an end in himself must as far as possible be my ends also, if that conception of an end in itself is to have its full effect in me.

This principle of humanity and of every rational nature generally as an end in itself is the supreme limiting condition of every man's freedom of 431 action. This principle is not borrowed from experience, first, because of its universality, inasmuch as it applies to all rational beings generally, and no experience is capable of determining anything about them; and, secondly, because in experience (subjectively) humanity is not thought of as the end of men, i.e., as an object that we of ourselves actually make our

---

23. Let it not be thought that the trivial *quod tibi non vis fieri, etc.* [do not do to others what you do not want done to yourself] can here serve as a standard or principle. For it is merely derived from our principle, although with several limitations. It cannot be a universal law, for it contains the ground neither of duties to oneself nor of duties of love toward others (for many a man would gladly consent that others should not benefit him, if only he might be excused from benefiting them). Nor, finally, does it contain the ground of strict duties toward others, for the criminal would on this ground be able to dispute with the judges who punish him; and so on.

end which as a law ought to constitute the supreme limiting condition of all subjective ends (whatever they may be); and hence this principle must arise from pure reason [and not from experience]. That is to say that the ground of all practical legislation lies objectively in the rule and in the form of universality, which (according to the first principle) makes the rule capable of being a law (say, for example, a law of nature). Subjectively, however, the ground of all practical legislation lies in the end; but (according to the second principle) the subject of all ends is every rational being as an end in himself. From this there now follows the third practical principle of the will as the supreme condition of the will's conformity with universal practical reason, viz. the idea of the will of every rational being as a will that legislates universal law.[24]

According to this principle all maxims are rejected which are not consistent with the will's own legislation of universal law. The will is thus not merely subject to the law but is subject to the law in such a way that it must be regarded also as legislating for itself and only on this account as being subject to the law (of which it can regard itself as the author).

In the previous formulations of imperatives, viz., that based on the conception of the conformity of actions to universal law in a way similar to a natural order and that based on the universal prerogative of rational beings as ends in themselves, these imperatives just because they were thought of as categorical excluded from their legislative authority all admixture of any interest as an incentive. They were, however, only assumed to be categorical because such an assumption had to be made if the concept of duty was to be explained. But that there were practical propositions which commanded categorically could not itself be proved, nor can it be proved anywhere in this section. But one thing could have been done, viz., to indicate that in willing from duty the renunciation of all interest is the specific mark distinguishing a categorical imperative from a hypothetical one and that such renunciation was expressed in the imperative itself by means of some determination contained in it. This is done in the present (third) formulation of the principle, namely, in the idea of the will of every rational being as a will that legislates universal law.

When such a will is thought of, then even though a will which is subject to law may be bound to this law by means of some interest, nevertheless a will that is itself a supreme lawgiver is not able as such to depend on any interest. For a will which is so dependent would itself require yet another law restricting the interest of its self-love to the condition that such interest should itself be valid as a universal law.

Thus the principle that every human will as a will that legislates universal law in all its maxims,[25] provided it is otherwise correct, would be well suited to being a categorical imperative in the following respect:

24. [This is usually called the formula of autonomy.]

25. I may here be excused from citing instances to elucidate this principle inasmuch as those which were first used to elucidate the categorical imperative and its formula can all serve the same purpose here. [See above Ak. 421–23, 429–30.]

just because of the idea of legislating universal law such an imperative is not based on any interest, and therefore it alone of all possible imperatives can be unconditional. Or still better, the proposition being converted, if there is a categorical imperative (i.e., a law for the will of every rational being), then it can only command that everything be done from the maxim of such a will as could at the same time have as its object only itself regarded as legislating universal law. For only then are the practical principle and the imperative which the will obeys unconditional, inasmuch as the will can be based on no interest at all.

When we look back upon all previous attempts that have been made to discover the principle of morality, there is no reason now to wonder why they one and all had to fail. Man was viewed as bound to laws by his duty; but it was not seen that man is subject only to his own, yet universal, legislation and that he is bound only to act in accordance with his own will, which is, however, a will purposed by nature to legislate universal laws. For when man is thought as being merely subject to a law (whatever it might be), then the law had to carry with it some interest 433 functioning as an attracting stimulus or as a constraining force for obedience, inasmuch as the law did not arise as a law from his own will. Rather, in order that his will conform with law, it had to be necessitated by something else to act in a certain way. By this absolutely necessary conclusion, however, all the labor spent in finding a supreme ground for duty was irretrievably lost; duty was never discovered, but only the necessity of acting from a certain interest. This might be either one's own interest or another's, but either way the imperative had to be always conditional and could never possibly serve as a moral command. I want, therefore, to call my principle the principle of the autonomy of the will, in contrast with every other principle, which I accordingly count under heteronomy.

The concept of every rational being as one who must regard himself as legislating universal law by all his will's maxims, so that he may judge himself and his actions from this point of view, leads to another very fruitful concept, which depends on the aforementioned one, viz., that of a kingdom of ends.

By "kingdom" I understand a systematic union of different rational beings through common laws. Now laws determine ends as regards their universal validity; therefore, if one abstracts from the personal differences of rational beings and also from all content of their private ends, then it will be possible to think of a whole of all ends in systematic connection (a whole both of rational beings as ends in themselves and also of the particular ends which each may set for himself); that is, one can think of a kingdom of ends that is possible on the aforesaid principles.

For all rational beings stand under the law that each of them should treat himself and all others never merely as means but always at the same time as an end in himself. Hereby arises a systematic union of rational beings through common objective laws, i.e., a kingdom that may be called a kingdom of ends (certainly only an ideal), inasmuch as these laws have in view the very relation of such beings to one another as ends and means.[26]

A rational being belongs to the kingdom of ends as a member when he legislates in it universal laws while also being himself subject to these laws. He belongs to it as sovereign, when as legislator he is himself subject to the will of no other.

434   A rational being must always regard himself as legislator in a kingdom of ends rendered possible by freedom of the will, whether as member or as sovereign. The position of the latter can be maintained not merely through the maxims of his will but only if he is a completely independent being without needs and with unlimited power adequate to his will.

Hence morality consists in the relation of all action to that legislation whereby alone a kingdom of ends is possible. This legislation must be found in every rational being and must be able to arise from his will, whose principle then is never to act on any maxim except such as can also be a universal law and hence such as the will can thereby regard itself as at the same time the legislator of universal law. If now the maxims do not by their very nature already necessarily conform with this objective principle of rational beings as legislating universal laws, then the necessity of acting on that principle is called practical necessitation, i.e., duty. Duty does not apply to the sovereign in the kingdom of ends, but it does apply to every member and to each in the same degree.

The practical necessity of acting according to this principle, i.e., duty, does not rest at all on feelings, impulses, and inclinations, but only on the relation of rational beings to one another, a relation in which the will of a rational being must always be regarded at the same time as legislative, because otherwise he could not be thought of as an end in himself. Reason, therefore, relates every maxim of the will as legislating universal laws to every other will and also to every action toward oneself; it does so not on account of any other practical motive or future advantage but rather from the idea of the dignity of a rational being who obeys no law except what he at the same time enacts himself.

In the kingdom of ends everything has either a price or a dignity. Whatever has a price can be replaced by something else as its equivalent; on the other hand, whatever is above all price, and therefore admits of no equivalent, has a dignity.

Whatever has reference to general human inclinations and needs has a market price; whatever, without presupposing any need, accords with a
435 certain taste, i.e., a delight in the mere unpurposive play of our mental powers,[27] has an affective price; but that which constitutes the condition under which alone something can be an end in itself has not merely a relative worth, i.e., a price, but has an intrinsic worth, i.e., dignity.

Now morality is the condition under which alone a rational being can be an end in himself, for only thereby can he be a legislating member in the kingdom of ends. Hence morality and humanity, insofar as it is

26. [This is usually called the formula of the kingdom of ends.]

27. [See Kant, *Critique of Aesthetic Judgment*, §'s 1–5.]

capable of morality, alone have dignity. Skill and diligence in work have a market price; wit, lively imagination, and humor have an affective price; but fidelity to promises and benevolence based on principles (not on instinct) have intrinsic worth. Neither nature nor art contain anything which in default of these could be put in their place; for their worth consists, not in the effects which arise from them, nor in the advantage and profit which they provide, but in mental dispositions, i.e., in the maxims of the will which are ready in this way to manifest themselves in action, even if they are not favored with success. Such actions also need no recommendation from any subjective disposition or taste so as to meet with immediate favor and delight; there is no need of any immediate propensity or feeling toward them. They exhibit the will performing them as an object of immediate respect; and nothing but reason is required to impose them upon the will, which is not to be cajoled into them, since in the case of duties such cajoling would be a contradiction. This estimation, therefore, lets the worth of such a disposition be recognized as dignity and puts it infinitely beyond all price, with which it cannot in the least be brought into competition or comparison without, as it were, violating its sanctity.

What then is it that entitles the morally good disposition, or virtue, to make such lofty claims? It is nothing less than the share which such a disposition affords the rational being of legislating universal laws, so that he is fit to be a member in a possible kingdom of ends, for which his own nature has already determined him as an end in himself and therefore as a legislator in the kingdom of ends. Thereby is he free as regards all laws of nature, and he obeys only those laws which he gives to himself. Accordingly, his maxims can belong to a universal legislation to which he at the same time subjects himself. For nothing can have any worth other than what the law determines. But the legislation itself which determines all worth must for that very reason have dignity, i.e., unconditional and incomparable worth; and the word "respect" alone provides a suitable expression for the esteem which a rational being must have for it. Hence autonomy is the ground of the dignity of human nature and of every rational nature. 436

The aforementioned three ways of representing the principle of morality are at bottom only so many formulas of the very same law: one of them by itself contains a combination of the other two. Nevertheless, there is a difference in them, which is subjectively rather than objectively practical, viz., it is intended to bring an idea of reason closer to intuition (in accordance with a certain analogy) and thereby closer to feeling. All maxims have, namely,

1. A form, which consists in universality; and in this respect the formula of the moral imperative is expressed thus: maxims must be so chosen as if they were to hold as universal laws of nature.

2. A matter, viz., an end; and here the formula says that a rational being, inasmuch as he is by his very nature an end and hence an end in himself, must serve in every maxim as a condition limiting all merely relative and arbitrary ends.

3. A complete determination of all maxims by the formula that all max-

ims proceeding from his own legislation ought to harmonize with a possible kingdom of ends as a kingdom of nature.[28] There is a progression here through the categories of the *unity* of the form of the will (its universality), the *plurality* of its matter (its objects, i.e., its ends), and the *totality* or completeness of its system of ends. But one does better if in moral judgment he follows the rigorous method and takes as his basis the universal formula of the categorical imperative: Act according to that maxim which can at the same time make itself a universal law. But if one wants also to secure acceptance for the moral law, it is very useful to bring one and the same action under the three aforementioned concepts and thus, as far as possible, to bring the moral law nearer to intuition.

We can now end where we started in the beginning, viz., the concept of an unconditionally good will. That will is absolutely good which cannot be evil, i.e., whose maxim, when made into a universal law, can never conflict with itself. This principle is therefore also its supreme law: Act always according to that maxim whose universality as a law you can at the same time will. This is the only condition under which a will can never be in conflict with itself, and such an imperative is categorical. Inasmuch as the validity of the will as a universal law for possible actions is analogous to the universal connection of the existence of things in accordance with universal laws, which is the formal aspect of nature in general, the categorical imperative can also be expressed thus: Act according to maxims which can at the same time have for their object themselves as universal laws of nature. Thus, then, the formula for an absolutely good will is constituted.

Rational nature is distinguished from the rest of nature by the fact that it sets itself an end. This end would be the matter of every good will. But in the idea of an absolutely good will—good without any qualifying condition (of attaining this or that end) —complete abstraction must be made from every end that has to come about as an effect (since such would make every will only relatively good). And so the end must here be conceived, not as an end to be effected, but as an independently existing end. Hence it must be conceived only negatively, i.e., as an end which should never be acted against and therefore as one which in all willing must never be regarded merely as means but must always be esteemed at the same time as an end. Now this end can be nothing but the subject of all possible ends themselves, because this subject is at the same time the subject of a possible absolutely good will; for such a will cannot without contradiction be subordinated to any other object. The principle: So act in regard to every rational being (yourself and others) that he may at the same time count in your maxim as an end in himself, is thus basically the same as the principle: Act on a maxim which at the same time contains in

437

438

28. Teleology considers nature as a kingdom of ends; morals regards a possible kingdom of ends as a kingdom of nature. In the former the kingdom of ends is a theoretical idea for explaining what exists. In the latter it is a practical idea for bringing about what does not exist but can be made actual by our conduct, i.e., what can be actualized in accordance with this very idea.

itself its own universal validity for every rational being. That in the use of means for every end my maxim should be restricted to the condition of its universal validity as a law for every subject says just the same as that a subject of ends, i.e., a rational being himself, must be made the ground for all maxims of actions and must thus be used never merely as means but as the supreme limiting condition in the use of all means, i.e., always at the same time as an end.

Now there follows incontestably from this that every rational being as an end in himself must be able to regard himself with reference to all laws to which he may be subject as being at the same time the legislator of universal law, for just this very fitness of his maxims for the legislation of universal law distinguishes him as an end in himself. There follows also that his dignity (prerogative) of being above all the mere things of nature implies that his maxims must be taken from the viewpoint that regards himself, as well as every other rational being, as being legislative beings (and hence are they called persons). In this way there is possible a world of rational beings (*mundus intelligibilis*) as a kingdom of ends, because of the legislation belonging to all persons as members. Therefore, every rational being must so act as if he were through his maxim always a legislating member in the universal kingdom of ends. The formal principle of these maxims is this: So act as if your maxims were to serve at the same time as a universal law (for all rational beings). Thus a kingdom of ends is possible only on the analogy of a kingdom of nature; yet the former is possible only through maxims, i.e., self-imposed rules, while the latter is possible only through laws of efficient causes necessitated from without. Regardless of this difference and even though nature as a whole is viewed as a machine, yet insofar as nature stands in a relation to rational beings as its ends, it is on this account given the name of a kingdom of nature. Such a kingdom of ends would actually be realized through maxims whose rule is prescribed to all rational beings by the categorical imperative, if these maxims were universally obeyed. But even if a rational being himself strictly obeys such a maxim, he cannot for that reason count on everyone else's being true to it, nor can he expect the kingdom of nature and its purposive order to be in harmony with him as a fitting member of a kingdom of ends made possible by himself, i.e., he cannot expect the kingdom of nature to favor his expectation of happiness. 439 Nevertheless, the law: Act in accordance with the maxims of a member legislating universal laws for a merely possible kingdom of ends, remains in full force, since it commands categorically. And just in this lies the paradox that merely the dignity of humanity as rational nature without any further end or advantage to be thereby gained—and hence respect for a mere idea—should yet serve as an inflexible precept for the will; and that just this very independence of the maxims from all such incentives should constitute the sublimity of maxims and the worthiness of every rational subject to be a legislative member in the kingdom of ends, for otherwise he would have to be regarded as subject only to the natural law of his own needs. And even if the kingdom of nature as well as the kingdom of ends were thought of as both united under one sovereign so that the latter kingdom would thereby no longer remain a mere idea but would acquire true reality, then indeed the kingdom of ends would gain the addition of a strong incentive, but never any increase in its intrinsic worth. For this sole absolute legislator must, in spite of all this, always be thought of as judging the worth of rational beings solely by the disinterested conduct prescribed to themselves by means of this idea alone. The essence of things is not altered by their external relations; and whatever without reference to such relations alone constitutes the absolute worth of man is also what he must be judged by, whoever the judge may be, even the Supreme Being. Hence morality is the relation of actions to the autonomy of the will, i.e., to the possible legislation of universal law by means of the maxims of the will. That action which is compatible with the autonomy of the will is permitted; that which is not compatible is forbidden. That will whose maxims are necessarily in accord with the laws of autonomy is a holy, or absolutely good, will. The dependence of a will which is not absolutely good upon the principle of autonomy (i.e., moral necessitation) is obligation, which cannot therefore be applied to a holy will. The objective necessity of an action from obligation is called duty.

From what has just been said, there can now easily be explained how it happens that, although in the concept of duty we think of subjection to the law, yet at the same time we thereby ascribe a certain dignity and sublimity to the person who fulfills all his duties. For not insofar as he is subject to the moral law does he have sublimity, but rather has it only insofar as with regard to this very same law he is at the same time legislative, and only thereby is he subject to the law. We have also shown above[29] how neither fear nor inclination, but solely respect for the law, is the incentive which can give an action moral worth. Our own will, insofar as it were to act only under the condition of its being able to legislate universal law by means of its maxims—this will, ideally possible for us, is the proper object of respect. And the dignity of humanity consists just in its capacity to legislate universal law, though with the condition of humanity's being at the same time itself subject to this very same legislation.

Autonomy of the Will
As the Supreme Principle of Morality

Autonomy of the will is the property that the will has of being a law to itself (independently of any property of the objects of volition). The principle of autonomy is this: Always choose in such a way that in the same volition the maxims of the choice are at the same time present as universal law. That this practical rule is an imperative, i.e., that the will of every rational being is necessarily bound to the rule as a condition, cannot be proved by merely analyzing the concepts contained in it, since it is a synthetic proposition. For proof one would have to go beyond cogni-

---

29. [Ak. 400–402.]

tion of objects to a critical examination of the subject, i.e. go to a critique of pure practical reason, since this synthetic proposition which commands apodeictically must be capable of being cognized completely a priori. This task, however, does not belong to the present section. But that the above principle of autonomy is the sole principle of morals can quite well be shown by mere analysis of the concepts of morality; for thereby the principle of morals is found to be necessarily a categorical imperative, which commands nothing more nor less than this very autonomy.

Heteronomy of the Will   441
As the Source of All Spurious Principles
of Morality

If the will seeks the law that is to determine it anywhere but in the fitness of its maxims for its own legislation of universal laws, and if it thus goes outside of itself and seeks this law in the character of any of its objects, then heteronomy always results. The will in that case does not give itself the law, but the object does so because of its relation to the will. This relation, whether it rests on inclination or on representations of reason, admits only of hypothetical imperatives: I ought to do something because I will something else. On the other hand, the moral, and hence categorical, imperative says that I ought to act in this way or that way, even though I did not will something else. For example, the former says that I ought not to lie if I would maintain my reputation; the latter says that I ought not to lie even though lying were to bring me not the slightest discredit. The moral imperative must therefore abstract from every object to such an extent that no object has any influence at all on the will, so that practical reason (the will) may not merely minister to an interest not belonging to it but may merely show its own commanding authority as the supreme legislation. Thus, for example, I ought to endeavor to promote the happiness of others, not as though its realization were any concern of mine (whether by immediate inclination or by any satisfaction indirectly gained through reason), but merely because a maxim which excludes it cannot be comprehended as a universal law in one and the same volition.

Classification of All Possible Principles of Morality
Founded upon the Assumed Fundamental Concept
of Heteronomy

Here as elsewhere human reason in its pure use, so long as it lacks a critical examination, first tried every possible wrong way before it succeeded in finding the only right way.

442 All principles that can be taken from this point of view are either empirical or rational. The first kind, drawn from the principle of happiness, are based upon either physical or moral feeling. The second kind, drawn from the principle of perfection, are based upon either the rational concept of perfection as a possible effect of our will or else upon the concept of an independent perfection (the will of God) as a determining cause of our will.

Empirical principles are wholly unsuited to serve as the foundation for moral laws. For the universality with which such laws ought to hold for all rational beings without exception (the unconditioned practical necessity imposed by moral laws upon such beings) is lost if the basis of these laws is taken from the particular constitution of human nature or from the accidental circumstances in which such nature is placed. But the principle of one's own happiness is the most objectionable. Such is the case not merely because this principle is false and because experience contradicts the supposition that well-being is always proportional to well-doing, nor yet merely because this principle contributes nothing to the establishment of morality, inasmuch as making a man happy is quite different from making him good and making him prudent and sharp-sighted for his own advantage quite different from making him virtuous. Rather, such is the case because this principle of one's own happiness bases morality upon incentives that undermine it rather than establish it and that totally destroy its sublimity, inasmuch as motives to virtue are put in the same class as motives to vice and inasmuch as such incentives merely teach one to become better at calculation, while the specific difference between virtue and vice is entirely obliterated. On the other hand, moral feeling, this alleged special sense,[30] remains closer to morality than does the aforementioned principle of one's own happiness. Yet the appeal to the principle of moral feeling is superficial, since men who cannot think believe that they will be helped out by feeling, even when the question is solely one of universal laws. They do so even though feelings naturally differ from one another by an infinity of degrees, so that feelings are not capable of providing a uniform measure of good and evil; furthermore, they do so even though one man cannot by his feeling judge validly at all for other men. Nevertheless, the principle of moral feeling is closer to morality and its dignity than is the principle of one's own happiness inasmuch as the former principle pays virtue the honor of ascribing to her directly the
443 satisfaction and esteem that is held for her, and does not, as it were, tell her to her face that our attachment to her rests not on her beauty but only on our advantage.

---

30. I count the principle of moral feeling under that of happiness, because every empirical interest promises to contribute to our well-being through the amenity afforded by something, whether immediately and without any reference to advantage or with reference to advantage. Similarly, the principle of sympathy for the happiness of others must with Hutcheson be counted along with the principle of moral sense as adopted by him. [Francis Hutcheson (1694–1747) was Professor of Moral Philosophy in the University of Glasgow, Scotland. He was the main proponent of the doctrine of moral sense.]

Among the rational principles of morality (or those arising from reason rather than from feeling) there is the ontological concept of perfection. It is empty, indeterminate, and hence of no use for finding in the immeasurable field of possible reality the maximum sum suitable for us. Furthermore, in attempting to distinguish specifically between the reality just mentioned and every other, it exhibits an inevitable tendency for turning about in a circle and cannot avoid tacitly presupposing the morality that it has to explain. Nevertheless, it is better than the theological concept, whereby morality is derived from a divine and most perfect will. It is better not merely because we cannot intuit divine perfection but can only derive it from our own concepts, among which morality is foremost; but also because if it is not so derived (and being thus derived would involve a crudely circular explanation), then the only remaining concept of God's will is drawn from such characteristics as desire for glory and dominion combined with such frightful representations as those of might and vengeance. Any system of morals based on such notions would be directly opposed to morality.

But if I had to choose between the concept of moral sense and that of perfection in general (both of which at least do not weaken morality, even though they are not at all capable of serving as its foundation), I would decide for the latter because it at least withdraws the decision of the question from sensibility and brings it to the court of pure reason, though it does not even here get any decision. Furthermore, I would choose the concept of perfection in general because it preserves the indeterminate idea (of a will good in itself) free from falsity until it can be more precisely determined.

For the rest, I believe that I may be excused from a lengthy refutation of all these doctrines. Such a refutation would be merely superfluous labor, since it is so easy and is presumably so well understood even by those whose office requires them to declare themselves for one of these theories (since their hearers would not tolerate suspension of judgment). But what interests us more here is to know that these principles never lay down anything but heteronomy of the will as the first ground of morality and that they must, consequently, necessarily fail in their purpose.

In every case where an object of the will must be laid down as the foundation for prescribing a rule to determine the will, there the rule is nothing but heteronomy. The imperative is then conditioned, viz., if or because one wills this object, one should act thus or so. Hence the imperative can never command morally, i.e., categorically. Now the object may determine the will by means of inclination, as in the case of the principle of one's own happiness, or by means of reason directed to objects of our volition in general, as in the case of the principle of perfection. Yet in both cases the will never determines itself immediately by the thought of an action, but only by the incentive that the anticipated effect of the action has upon the will: I ought to do something because I will something else. And here must yet another law be assumed in me the subject, whereby I necessarily will this something else; this other law in turn requires an imperative to restrict this maxim. For the impulse which the representation of an object that is possible by means of our powers is to exert upon the will of a subject in accordance with his natural constitution belongs to the nature of the subject, whether to his sensibility (his inclination and taste) or to his understanding and reason, whose employment on an object is by the particular arrangement of their nature attended with satisfaction; consequently, the law would, properly speaking, be given by nature. This law, insofar as it is a law of nature, must be known and proved through experience and is therefore in itself contingent and hence is not fit to be an apodeictic practical rule, such as a moral rule must be. The law of nature under discussion is always merely heteronomy of the will; the will does not give itself the law, but a foreign impulse gives the law to the will by means of the subject's nature, which is adapted to receive such an impulse.

An absolutely good will, whose principle must be a categorical imperative, will therefore be indeterminate as regards all objects and will contain merely the form of willing; and indeed that form is autonomy. This is to say that the fitness of the maxims of every good will to make themselves universal laws is itself the only law that the will of every rational being imposes on itself, without needing to assume any incentive or interest as a basis.

How such a synthetic practical a priori proposition is possible and why it is necessary are problems whose solution does not lie any longer within the bounds of a metaphysics of morals. Furthermore, we have not here 445 asserted the truth of this proposition, much less professed to have within our power a proof of it. We simply showed by developing the universally accepted concept of morality that autonomy of the will is unavoidably bound up with it, or rather is its very foundation. Whoever, then, holds morality to be something real, and not a chimerical idea without any truth, must also admit the principle here put forward. Hence this section, like the first, was merely analytic. To show that morality is not a mere phantom of the brain, which morality cannot be if the categorical imperative, and with it the autonomy of the will, is true and absolutely necessary as an a priori principle, we require a possible synthetic use of pure practical reason. But we must not venture on this use without prefacing it with a critical examination of this very faculty of reason. In the last section we shall give the main outlines of this critical examination as far as sufficient for our purpose.[31]

31. [The ensuing Third Section is difficult to grasp. Kant expressed himself more clearly regarding the topics discussed there in the *Critique of Practical Reason*, Part I, Book I ("Analytic of Pure Practical Reason").]

TRANSITION FROM A METAPHYSICS OF MORALS TO A
CRITIQUE OF PURE PRACTICAL REASON

*The Concept of Freedom Is the Key for an Explanation
of the Autonomy of the Will*

The will is a kind of causality belonging to living beings insofar as they are rational; freedom would be the property of this causality that makes it effective independent of any determination by alien causes. Similarly, natural necessity is the property of the causality of all non-rational beings by which they are determined to activity through the influence of alien causes.

The foregoing explanation of freedom is negative and is therefore unfruitful for attaining an insight regarding its essence; but there arises from it a positive concept, which as such is richer and more fruitful. The concept of causality involves that of laws according to which something that we call cause must entail something else—namely, the effect. Therefore freedom is certainly not lawless, even though it is not a property of will in accordance with laws of nature. It must, rather, be a causality in accordance with immutable laws, which, to be sure, is of a special kind; otherwise a free will would be something absurd. As we have already seen [in the preceding paragraph], natural necessity is a heteronomy of efficient causes, inasmuch as every effect is possible only in accordance with the law that something 447 else determines the efficient cause to exercise its causality. What else, then, can freedom of the will be but autonomy, i.e., the property that the will has of being a law to itself? The proposition that the will is in every action a law to itself expresses, however, nothing but the principle of acting according to no other maxim than that which can at the same time have itself as a universal law for its object. Now this is precisely the formula of the categorical imperative and is the principle of morality. Thus a free will and a will subject to moral laws are one and the same.

Therefore if freedom of the will is presupposed, morality (together with its principle) follows by merely analyzing the concept of freedom. However, the principle of morality is, nevertheless, a synthetic proposition: viz., an absolutely good will is one whose maxim can always have itself as content when such maxim is regarded as a universal law; it is synthetic because this property of the will's maxim can never be found by analyzing the concept of an absolutely good will. Now such synthetic propositions are possible only as follows—two cognitions are bound together through their connection with a third in which both of them are to be found. The positive concept of freedom furnishes this third cognition, which cannot, as is the case with physical causes, be the nature of the world of sense (in whose concept is combined the concept of something as cause in relation to something else as effect). We cannot here yet show straight away what this third cognition is which freedom indicates to us and of which we have an a priori idea, nor can we as yet conceive of the deduction of the concept of freedom from pure practical reason and therewith also the possibility of a categorical imperative. Rather, we require some further preparation.

Freedom Must Be Presupposed as a Property of the Will of All Rational Beings

It is not enough to ascribe freedom to our will, on whatever ground, if we have not also sufficient reason for attributing it to all rational beings. For inasmuch as morality serves as a law for us only insofar as we are rational beings, it must also be valid for all rational beings. And since morality must be derived solely from the property of freedom, one must show that freedom is also the property of the will of all rational beings. It 448 is not enough to prove freedom from certain alleged experiences of human nature (such a proof is indeed absolutely impossible, and so freedom can be proved only a priori). Rather, one must show that freedom belongs universally to the activity of rational beings endowed with a will. Now I say that every being which cannot act in any way other than under the idea of freedom is for this very reason free from a practical point of view. This is to say that for such a being all the laws that are inseparably bound up with freedom are valid just as much as if the will of such a being could be declared to be free in itself for reasons that are valid for theoretical philosophy.[1] Now I claim that we must necessarily attribute to every rational being who has a will also the idea of freedom, under which only can such a being act. For in such a being we think of a reason that is practical, i.e., that has causality in reference to its objects. Now we cannot possibly think of a reason that consciously lets itself be directed from outside as regards its judgments; for in that case the subject would ascribe the determination of his faculty of judgment not to his reason, but to an impulse. Reason must regard itself as the author of its principles independent of foreign influences. Therefore as practical reason or as the will of a rational being must reason regard itself as free. This is to say that the will of a rational being can be a will of its own only under the idea of freedom, and that such a will must therefore, from a practical point of view, be attributed to all rational beings.

1. I adopt this method of assuming as sufficient for our purpose that freedom is presupposed merely as an idea by rational beings in their actions in order that I may avoid the necessity of having to prove freedom from a theoretical point of view as well. For even if this latter problem is left unresolved, the same laws that would bind a being who was really free are valid equally for a being who cannot act otherwise than under the idea of its own freedom. Thus we can relieve ourselves of the burden which presses on the theory.

Concerning the Interest Attached
to the Ideas of Morality

We have finally traced the determinate concept of morality back to the idea of freedom, but we could not prove freedom to be something actual in ourselves and in human nature. We saw merely that we must presuppose it if we want to think of a being as rational and as endowed with consciousness of its causality as regards actions, i.e., as endowed with a will. And so we find that on the very same ground we must attribute to every being endowed with reason and a will this property of determining itself to action under the idea of its own freedom. 449

Now there resulted from the presupposition of this idea of freedom also the consciousness of a law of action: that the subjective principles of actions, i.e., maxims, must always be so adopted that they can also be valid objectively, i.e., universally, as principles, and can therefore serve as universal laws of our own legislation. But why, then, should I subject myself to this principle simply as a rational being and by so doing also subject to this principle all other beings endowed with reason? I am willing to grant that no interest impels me to do so, because this would not give a categorical imperative. But nonetheless I must necessarily take an interest in it and discern how this comes about, for this *ought* is properly a *would* which is valid for every rational being, provided that reason is practical for such a being without hindrances. In the case of beings who, like ourselves, are also affected by sensibility, i.e., by incentives of a kind other than the purely rational, and who do not always act as reason by itself would act, this necessity of action is expressed only as an *ought*, and the subjective necessity is to be distinguished from the objective.

It therefore seems as if we have in the idea of freedom actually only presupposed the moral law, namely, the principle of the autonomy of the will, and as if we could not prove its reality and objective necessity independently. In that case we should indeed still have gained something quite considerable by at least determining the genuine principle more exactly than had previously been done. But as regards its validity and the practical necessity of subjecting oneself to it, we would have made no progress. We could give no satisfactory answer if asked the following questions: why must the universal validity of our maxim taken as a law be a condition restricting our actions; upon what do we base the worth that we assign to this way of acting—a worth that is supposed to be so great that there can be no higher interest; how does it happen that by this alone does man believe that he feels his own personal worth, in comparison 450 with which that of an agreeable or disagreeable condition is to be regarded as nothing.

Indeed we do sometimes find that we can take an interest in a personal characteristic which involves no interest in any [external] condition but only makes us capable of participating in the condition in case reason were to effect the allotment. This is to say that the mere worthiness of being happy can of itself be of interest even without the motive of participating in this happiness. This judgment, however, is in fact only the result of the importance that we have already presupposed as belonging to moral laws (when by the idea of freedom we divorce ourselves from all empirical interest). However, in this way we are not as yet able to have any insight into why it is that we should divorce ourselves from such interest, i.e., that we should consider ourselves as free in action and yet hold ourselves as subject to certain laws so as to find solely in our own person a worth that can compensate us for the loss of everything that gives worth to our condition. We do not see how this is possible and hence how the moral law can obligate us.

One must frankly admit that there is here a sort of circle from which, so it seems, there is no way to escape. In the order of efficient causes we assume that we are free so that we may think of ourselves as subject to moral laws in the order of ends. And we then think of ourselves as subject to these laws because we have attributed to ourselves freedom of the will. Freedom and self-legislation of the will are both autonomy and are hence reciprocal concepts. Since they are reciprocal, one of them cannot be used to explain the other or to supply its ground, but can at most be used only for logical purposes to bring seemingly different conceptions of the same object under a single concept (just as different fractions of the same value are reduced to lowest terms).

However, one recourse still remains open to us, namely, to inquire whether we do not take one point of view when by means of freedom we think of ourselves as a priori efficient causes, and another point of view when we represent ourselves with reference to our actions as effects which we see before our eyes.

No subtle reflection is required for the following observation, which even the commonest understanding may be supposed to make, though it does so in its own fashion through some obscure discrimination of the faculty of judgment which it calls feeling: all representations that come to us without our choice (such as those of the senses) enable us to know objects only as they affect us; what they may be in themselves remains unknown to us. Therefore, even with the closest attention and the greatest clarity that the understanding can bring to such representations, we can attain to a mere knowledge of appearances but never to knowledge of things in themselves. Once this distinction is made (perhaps merely as a result of observing the difference between representations which are given to us from without and in which we are passive from those which we produce entirely from ourselves and in which we show our own activity), then there follows of itself that we must admit and assume that behind the appearances there is something else which is not appearance, namely, things in themselves. Inasmuch as we can never cognize them except as they affect us [through our senses], we must admit that we can never come any nearer to them nor ever know what they are in themselves. This must provide a distinction, however crude, between a world of sense and a world of understanding; the former can vary considerably according to the difference of sensibility [and sense impressions]

451

in various observers, while the latter, which is the basis of the former, remains always the same. Even with regard to himself, a man cannot presume to know what he is in himself by means of the acquaintance which he has through internal sensation. For since he does not, as it were, create himself and since he acquires the concept of himself not a priori but empirically, it is natural that he can attain knowledge even about himself only through inner sense and therefore only through the appearance of his nature and the way in which his consciousness is affected. But yet he must necessarily assume that beyond his own subject's constitution as composed of nothing but appearances there must be something else as basis, namely, his ego as constituted in itself. Therefore with regard to mere perception and the receptivity of sensations, he must count himself as belonging to the world of sense; but with regard to whatever there may be in him of pure activity (whatever reaches consciousness immediately and not through affecting the senses) he must count himself as belonging to the intellectual world, of which he has, however, no further knowledge.

Such a conclusion must be reached by a reflective man regarding all the things that may be presented to him. It is presumably to be found even in 452 the most ordinary understanding, which, as is well known, is quite prone to expect that behind objects of the senses there is something else invisible and acting of itself. But such understanding spoils all this by making the invisible again sensible, i.e., it wants to make the invisible an object of intuition; and thereby does it become not a bit wiser.

Now man really finds in himself a faculty which distinguishes him from all other things and even from himself insofar as he is affected by objects. That faculty is reason, which as pure spontaneity is elevated even above understanding. For although the latter is also spontaneous and does not, like sense, merely contain representations that arise only when one is affected by things (and is therefore passive), yet understanding can produce by its activity no other concepts than those which merely serve to bring sensuous representations [intuitions] under rules and thereby to unite them in one consciousness. Without this use of sensibility, understanding would think nothing at all. Reason, on the other hand, shows such a pure spontaneity in the case of what are called ideas that it goes far beyond anything that sensibility can offer and shows its highest occupation in distinguishing the world of sense from the world of understanding, thereby prescribing limits to the understanding itself.

Therefore a rational being must regard himself qua intelligence (and hence not from the side of his lower powers) as belonging not to the world of sense but to the world of understanding. Therefore he has two standpoints from which he can regard himself and know laws of the use of his powers and hence of all his actions: first, insofar as he belongs to the world of sense subject to laws of nature (heteronomy); secondly, insofar as he belongs to the intelligible world subject to laws which, independent of nature, are not empirical but are founded only on reason.

As a rational being and hence as belonging to the intelligible world, can man never think of the causality of his own will except under the idea of

freedom; for independence from the determining causes of the world of sense (an independence which reason must always attribute to itself) is freedom. Now the idea of freedom is inseparably connected with the concept of autonomy, and this in turn with the universal principle of morali-
453 ty, which ideally is the ground of all actions of rational beings, just as natural law is the ground of all appearances.

The suspicion that we raised earlier is now removed, viz., that there might be a hidden circle involved in our inference from freedom to autonomy, and from this to the moral law—this is to say that we had perhaps laid down the idea of freedom only for the sake of the moral law in order subsequently to infer this law in its turn from freedom, and that we had therefore not been able to assign any ground at all for this law but had only assumed it by begging a principle which well-disposed souls would gladly concede us but which we could never put forward as a demonstrable proposition. But now we see that when we think of ourselves as free, we transfer ourselves into the intelligible world as members and know the autonomy of the will together with its consequence, morality; whereas when we think of ourselves as obligated, we consider ourselves as belonging to the world of sense and yet at the same time to the intelligible world.

How Is a Categorical Imperative Possible?

The rational being counts himself, qua intelligence, as belonging to the intelligible world, and only insofar as he is an efficient cause belonging to the intelligible world does he call his causality a will. But on the other side, he is conscious of himself as being also a part of the world of sense, where his actions are found as mere appearances of that causality. The possibility of these actions cannot, however, be discerned through such causality, which we do not know; rather, these actions as belonging to the world of sense must be viewed as determined by other appearances, namely, desires and inclinations. Therefore, if I were solely a member of the intelligible world, then all my actions would perfectly conform to the principle of the autonomy of a pure will; if I were solely a part of the world of sense, my actions would have to be taken as in complete conformity with the natural law of desires and inclinations, i.e., with the heteronomy of nature. (My actions would in the first case rest on the supreme principle of morality, in the second case on that of happiness.) But the intelligible world contains the ground of the world of sense and therefore also the ground of its laws; consequently, the intelligible world is (and must be thought of as) directly legislative for my will (which belongs wholly to the intelligible world). Therefore, even though on the one hand I must regard myself as a being belonging to the world of sense, yet on the other hand shall I have to know myself as an intelligence and as
454 subject to the law of the intelligible world, i.e., to reason, which contains

this law in the idea of freedom, and hence to know myself as subject to the autonomy of the will. Consequently, I must regard the laws of the intelligible world as imperatives for me, and the actions conforming to this principle as duties.

And thus are categorical imperatives possible because the idea of freedom makes me a member of an intelligible world. Now if I were a member of only that world, all my actions *would* always accord with autonomy of the will. But since I intuit myself at the same time as a member of the world of sense, my actions *ought* so to accord. This categorical *ought* presents a synthetic a priori proposition, whereby in addition to my will as affected by sensuous desires there is added further the idea of the same will, but as belonging to the intelligible world, pure and practical of itself, and as containing the supreme condition of the former will insofar as reason is concerned. All this is similar to the way in which concepts [categories] of the understanding, which of themselves signify nothing but the form of law in general, are added to intuitions of the world of sense and thus make possible synthetic a priori propositions, upon which all knowledge of nature rests.

The practical use of ordinary human reason bears out the correctness of this deduction. There is no one, not even the meanest villain, provided only that he is otherwise accustomed to the use of reason, who, when presented with examples of honesty of purpose, of steadfastness in following good maxims, and of sympathy and general benevolence (even when involved with great sacrifices of advantages and comfort) does not wish that he might also possess these qualities. Yet he cannot attain these in himself only because of his inclinations and impulses; but at the same time he wishes to be free from such inclinations which are a burden to him. He thereby proves that by having a will free of sensuous impulses he transfers himself in thought into an order of things entirely different from that of his desires in the field of sensibility. Since he cannot expect to obtain by the aforementioned wish any gratification of his desires or any condition that would satisfy any of his actual or even conceivable inclinations (inasmuch as through such an expectation the very idea that elicited the wish would be deprived of its preëminence) he can only expect a greater intrinsic worth of his own person. This better person he believes himself to be when he transfers himself to the standpoint of a   455 member of the intelligible world, to which he is involuntarily forced by the idea of freedom, i.e., of being independent of determination by causes of the world of sense. From this standpoint he is conscious of having a good will, which by his own admission constitutes the law for the bad will belonging to him as a member of the world of sense—a law whose authority he acknowledges even while he transgresses it. The moral *ought* is, therefore, a necessary *would* insofar as he is a member of the intelligible world, and is thought by him as an *ought* only insofar as he regards himself as being at the same time a member of the world of sense.

Concerning the Extreme Limit of All Practical Philosophy

All men think of themselves as free as far as their will is concerned. Hence arise all judgments upon actions as being such as ought to have been done, even though they were not done. But this freedom is not a concept of experience, nor can it be such, since it always holds, even though experience shows the opposite of those requirements represented as necessary under the presupposition of freedom. On the other hand, it is just as necessary that whatever happens should be determined without any exception according to laws of nature; and this necessity of nature is likewise no concept of experience, just because it involves the concept of necessity and thus of a priori knowledge. But this concept of nature is confirmed by experience and must inevitably be presupposed if there is to be possible experience, which is coherent knowledge of the objects of sense in accordance with universal laws. Freedom is, therefore, only an idea of reason whose objective reality is in itself questionable; but nature is a concept of the understanding, which proves, and necessarily must prove, its reality by examples from experience.

There arises from this a dialectic of reason, since the freedom attributed to the will seems to contradict the necessity of nature. And even though at this parting of the ways reason for speculative purposes finds the road of natural necessity much better worn and more serviceable than that of freedom, yet for practical purposes the footpath of freedom is the only one upon which it is possible to make use of reason in our conduct. Therefore, it is just as impossible for the most subtle philosophy as for the most ordinary human reason to argue away freedom. Hence philosophy must assume that no real contradiction will be found between freedom and natural necessity in the same human actions, for it cannot give up the concept of nature any more than that of freedom.

Nevertheless, even though one might never be able to comprehend how freedom is possible, yet this apparent contradiction must at least be removed in a convincing manner. For if the thought of freedom contradicts itself or nature, which is equally necessary, then freedom would have to be completely given up in favor of natural necessity.

It would, however, be impossible to escape this contradiction if the subject, deeming himself free, were to think of himself in the same sense or in the very same relationship when he calls himself free as when he assumes himself subject to the law of nature regarding the same action. Therefore, an unavoidable problem of speculative philosophy is at least to show that its illusion regarding the contradiction rests on our thinking of man in a different sense and relation when we call him free from when we regard him as being a part of nature and hence as subject to the laws of nature. Hence it must show not only that both can coexist very well, but that both must be thought of as necessarily united in the same subject; for otherwise no explanation could be given as to why reason should be burdened with an idea which involves us in a perplexity that is sorely embarrassing to reason in its theoretic use, even though it may without con-

456

tradiction be united with another idea that is sufficiently established. This duty, however, is incumbent solely on speculative philosophy in order that it may clear the way for practical philosophy. Thus the philosopher has no option as to whether he will remove the apparent contradiction or leave it untouched; for in the latter case the theory regarding this could be *bonum vacans*,[2] into the possession of which the fatalist can justifiably enter and chase all morality out of its supposed property as occupying it without title.

Nevertheless, one cannot here say as yet that the boundary of practical philosophy begins. For the settlement of the controversy does not belong to practical philosophy; the latter only requires speculative reason to put an end to the dissension in which it is entangled as regards theoretical 457 questions in order that practical reason may have rest and security from external attacks that might make disputable the ground upon which it wants to build.

The just claim to freedom of the will made even by ordinary human reason is founded on the consciousness and the admitted presupposition that reason is independent of mere subjective determination by causes which together make up what belongs only to sensation and comes under the general designation of sensibility. Regarding himself in this way as intelligence, man thereby puts himself into another order of things. And when he thinks of himself as intelligence endowed with a will and consequently with causality, he puts himself into relation with determining grounds of a kind altogether different from the kind when he perceives himself as a phenomenon in the world of sense (as he really is also) and subjects his causality to external determination according to laws of nature. Now he soon realizes that both can—and indeed must—hold good at the same time. For there is not the slightest contradiction involved in saying that a thing as appearance (belonging to the world of sense) is subject to certain laws, while it is independent of those laws when regarded as a thing or being in itself. That man must represent and think of himself in this two-fold way rests, on the one hand, upon the consciousness of himself as an object affected through the senses and, on the other hand, upon the consciousness of himself as intelligence, i.e., as independent of sensuous impulses in his use of reason (and hence as belonging to the intelligible world).

And hence man claims that he has a will which reckons to his account nothing that belongs merely to his desires and inclinations, and which, on the contrary, thinks of actions that can be performed only by disregarding all desires and sensuous incitements as being possible and as indeed being necessary for him. The causality of such actions lies in man as intelligence and lies in the laws of such effects and actions as are in accordance with principles of an intelligible world, of which he knows nothing more than that in such a world reason alone, and indeed pure reason independent of sensibility, gives the law. Furthermore, since he is in such a world his

2. [vacant property]

proper self only as intelligence (whereas regarded as a human being he is merely an appearance of himself), those laws apply to him immediately and categorically. Consequently, incitements from inclinations and impulses (and hence from the whole nature of the world of sense) cannot impair the laws of his willing insofar as he is intelligence. Indeed he does not even hold himself responsible for such inclinations and impulses or ascribe them to his proper self, i.e., his will, although he does ascribe to his will any indulgence which he might extend to them if he allowed them any influence on his maxims to the detriment of the rational laws of his will.

458

When practical reason thinks itself into an intelligible world, it does not in the least thereby transcend its limits, as it would if it tried to enter it by intuition or sensation. The thought of an intelligible world is merely negative as regards the world of sense. The latter world does not give reason any laws for determining the will and is positive only in this single point, viz., it simultaneously combines freedom as negative determination with a positive faculty and even a causality of reason. This causality is designated as a will to act in such a way that the principle of actions may accord with the essential character of a rational cause, i.e., with the condition that the maxim of these actions have universal validity as a law. But if practical reason were to bring in an object of the will, i.e., a motive of action, from the intelligible world, then it would overstep its boundaries and pretend to be acquainted with something of which it knows nothing. The concept of an intelligible world is thus only a point of view which reason sees itself compelled to take outside of appearances in order to think of itself as practical. If the influences of sensibility were determining for man, reason would not be able to take this point of view, which is nonetheless necessary if he is not to be denied the consciousness of himself as intelligence and hence as a rational cause that is active through reason, i.e., free in its operation. This thought certainly involves the idea of an order and a legislation different from that of the mechanism of nature which applies to the world of sense; and it makes necessary the concept of an intelligible world (i.e., the whole of rational beings as things in themselves). But it makes not the slightest claim to anything more than to think of such a world as regards merely its formal condition—i.e., the universality of the will's maxims as laws and thus the will's autonomy, which alone is consistent with freedom. On the contrary, all laws determined by reference to an object yield heteronomy, which can be found only in laws of nature and can apply only to the world of sense.

459

But reason would overstep all its bounds if it undertook to explain how pure reason can be practical. This is exactly the same problem as explaining how freedom is possible.

For we can explain nothing but what we can reduce to laws whose object can be given in some possible experience. But freedom is a mere idea, whose objective reality can in no way be shown in accordance with laws of nature and consequently not in any possible experience. Therefore, the idea of freedom can never admit of comprehension or even of insight, because it cannot by any analogy have an example falling under it. It holds only as a necessary presupposition of reason in a being who believes himself conscious of a will, i.e., of a faculty distinct from mere desire (namely, a faculty of determining himself to action as intelligence and hence in accordance with laws of reason independently of natural instincts). But where determination according to laws of nature ceases, there likewise ceases all explanation and nothing remains but defense, i.e., refutation of the objections of those who profess to have seen deeper into the essence of things and thereupon boldly declare freedom to be impossible. One can only show them that their supposed discovery of a contradiction lies nowhere but here: in order to make the law of nature applicable to human actions, they have necessarily had to regard man as an appearance; and now when they are required to think of man qua intelligence as thing in himself as well, they still persist in regarding him as appearance. In that case, to be sure, the exemption of man's causality (i.e., his will) from all the natural laws of the world of sense would, as regards one and the same subject, give rise to a contradiction. But this disappears if they would but bethink themselves and admit, as is reasonable, that behind appearances there must lie as their ground also things in themselves (though hidden) and that the laws of their operations cannot be expected to be the same as those that govern their appearances.

The subjective impossibility of explaining freedom of the will is the same as the impossibility of discovering and explaining an interest[3] which man 460 can take in moral laws. Nevertheless, he does indeed take such an interest, the basis of which in us is called moral feeling. Some people have falsely construed this feeling to be the standard of our moral judgment, whereas it must rather be regarded as the subjective effect that the law exercises upon the will, while reason alone furnishes the objective grounds of such moral feeling.

In order to will what reason alone prescribes as an *ought* for sensuously affected rational beings, there certainly must be a power of reason to infuse a feeling of pleasure or satisfaction in the fulfillment of duty, and hence there has to be a causality of reason to determine sensibility in accordance with rational principles. But it is quite impossible to discern, i.e., to make a priori conceivable, how a mere thought which itself contains nothing sensuous can produce a sensation of pleasure or displeasure. For here is a special kind of causality regarding which, as with all causali-

---

3. Interest is that by which reason becomes practical, i.e., a cause determining the will. Therefore one says of rational beings only that they take an interest in something; nonrational creatures feel only sensuous impulses. Reason takes an immediate interest in the action only when the universal validity of the maxim of the action is a sufficient determining ground of the will. Such an interest alone is pure. But when reason is able to determine the will only by means of another object of desire or under the presupposition of some special feeling in the subject, then reason takes only a mediate interest in the action. And since reason of itself alone without the help of experience can discover neither objects of the will nor a special feeling underlying the will, the latter interest would be only empirical and not a pure rational interest. The logical interest of reason (viz., to extend its insights) is never immediate, but presupposes purposes for which reason might be used.

ty, we can determine nothing a priori but must consult experience alone. However, experience can provide us with no relation of cause and effect except between two objects of experience. But in this case pure reason by means of mere ideas (which furnish no object at all for experience) is to be the cause of an effect that admittedly lies in experience. Consequently, there is for us men no possibility at all for an explanation as to how and why the universality of a maxim as a law, and hence morality, interests us. This much only is certain: the moral law is valid for us not because it interests us (for this is heteronomy and the dependence of practical reason 461 on sensibility, viz., on an underlying feeling whereby reason could never be morally legislative); but, rather, the moral law interests us because it is valid for us as men, since it has sprung from our will as intelligence and hence from our proper self. But what belongs to mere appearance is necessarily subordinated by reason to the nature of the thing in itself.

Thus the question as to how a categorical imperative is possible can be answered to the extent that there can be supplied the sole presupposition under which such an imperative is alone possible—namely, the idea of freedom. The necessity of this presupposition is discernible, and this much is sufficient for the practical use of reason, i.e., for being convinced as to the validity of this imperative, and hence also of the moral law; but how this presupposition itself is possible can never be discerned by any human reason. However, on the presupposition of freedom of the will of an intelligence, there necessarily follows the will's autonomy as the formal condition under which alone the will can be determined. To presuppose this freedom of the will (without involving any contradiction with the principle of natural necessity in the connection of appearances in the world of sense) is not only quite possible (as speculative philosophy can show), but is without any further condition also necessary for a rational being conscious of his causality through reason and hence conscious of a will (which is different from desires) as he makes such freedom in practice, i.e., in idea, the underlying condition of all his voluntary actions. But how pure reason can be practical by itself without other incentives taken from whatever source—i.e., how the mere principle of the universal validity of all reason's maxims as laws (which would certainly be the form of a pure practical reason) can by itself, without any matter (object) of the will in which some antecedent interest might be taken, furnish an incentive and produce an interest which could be called purely moral; or, in other words, how pure reason could be practical: to explain all this is quite beyond the power of human reason, and all the effort and work of seeking such an explanation is wasted.

It is just the same as if I tried to find out how freedom itself is possible as 462 causality of a will. For I thereby leave the philosophical basis of explanation, and I have no other basis. Now I could indeed flutter about in the world of intelligences, i.e., in the intelligible world still remaining to me. But even though I have an idea of such a world—an idea which has its own good grounds—yet I have not the slightest acquaintance with such a world and can never attain such acquaintance by all the efforts of my natural faculty of reason. This intelligible world signifies only a something that remains over when I have excluded from the determining grounds of my will everything that belongs to the world of sense, so as to restrict the principle of having all motives come from the field of sensibility. By so doing I set bounds to this field and show that it does not contain absolutely everything within itself but that beyond it there is still something more, regarding which, however, I have no further acquaintance. After the exclusion of all matter, i.e., cognition of objects, from pure reason which thinks this ideal, nothing remains over for me except such reason's form, viz., the practical law of the universal validity of maxims; and in conformity with this law I think of reason in its relation to a pure intelligible world as a possible efficient cause, i.e., as a cause determining the will. An incentive must in this case be wholly absent; this idea of an intelligible world would here have to be itself the incentive or have to be that in which reason originally took an interest. But to make this conceivable is precisely the problem that we cannot solve.

Here then is the extreme limit of all moral inquiry. To determine this limit is of great importance for the following considerations. On the one hand, reason should not, to the detriment of morals, search around in the world of sense for the supreme motive and for some interest that is conceivable but is nonetheless empirical. On the other hand, reason should not flap its wings impotently, without leaving the spot, in a space that for it is empty, namely, the space of transcendent concepts that is called the intelligible world, and thereby lose itself among mere phantoms of the brain. Furthermore, the idea of a pure intelligible world regarded as a whole of all intelligences to which we ourselves belong as rational beings (even though we are from another standpoint also members of the world of sense) remains always a useful and permissible idea for the purpose of a rational belief, although all knowledge ends at its boundary. This idea produces in us a lively interest in the moral law by means of the splendid ideal of a universal kingdom of ends in themselves (rational beings), to which we can belong as members only if we carefully conduct ourselves 463 according to maxims of freedom as if they were laws of nature.

Concluding Remark

The speculative use of reason with regard to nature leads to the absolute necessity of some supreme cause of the world. The practical use of reason with reference to freedom leads also to absolute necessity, but only to the necessity of the laws of the actions of a rational being as such. Now it is an essential principle of all use of our reason to push its knowledge to a consciousness of its necessity (for without necessity there would be no rational knowledge). But there is an equally essential restriction of the same reason that it cannot have insight into the necessity either of what is or what does happen or of what should happen, unless there is presupposed a condition under which it is or does happen or should happen. In this way, however, the satisfaction of reason is only further and further postponed by the continual inquiry after the condition. Reason, therefore, restlessly seeks the unconditionally necessary and sees itself compelled to assume this without having any means of making such necessity conceivable; reason is happy enough if only it can find a concept which is compatible with this assumption. Hence there is no fault in our deduction of the supreme principle of morality, but rather a reproach which must be made against human reason generally, involved in the fact that reason cannot render conceivable the absolute necessity of an unconditioned practical law (such as the categorical imperative must be). Reason cannot be blamed for not being willing to explain this necessity by means of a condition, namely, by basing it on some underlying interest, because in that case the law would no longer be moral, i.e., a supreme law of freedom. And so even though we do not indeed grasp the practical unconditioned necessity of the moral imperative, we do nevertheless grasp its inconceivability. This is all that can be fairly asked of a philosophy which strives in its principles to reach the very limit of human reason.

SUPPLEMENT

ON A SUPPOSED RIGHT TO LIE
BECAUSE OF PHILANTHROPIC CONCERNS[1]

In the periodical *France*[2] for 1797, Part VI, No. 1, page 123, in an article bearing the title "On Political Reactions"[3] by Benjamin Constant[4] there is contained on p. 123 the following passage:

"The moral principle stating that it is a duty to tell the truth would make any society impossible if that principle were taken singly and unconditionally. We have proof of this in the very direct consequences which a German philosopher has drawn from this principle. This philosopher goes as far as to assert that it would be a crime to tell a lie to a murderer who asked whether our friend who is being pursued by the murderer had taken refuge in our house."[5]

The French philosopher [Constant] on p. 124 [of the periodical *France*] refutes this [moral] principle in the following way:

"It is a duty to tell the truth. The concept of duty is inseparable from the concept of right. A duty is what in one man corresponds to the right of another. Where there are

1. [This essay appeared in September of 1799 in *Berlinische Blätter (Berlin Press)*, published by Biester. See H. J. Paton, "An Alleged Right to Lie" in *Kant-Studien* 45 (1953–54).]

2. [The periodical *Frankreich im Jahre 1797. Aus den Briefen deutscher Männer in Paris* (*France in the Year 1797. From Letters of German Men in Paris*), published in Altona.]

3. [*Des réactions politiques* had appeared in May of 1796, and it was translated into German in this periodical *Frankreich*.]

4. [Henri Benjamin Constant de Rebecque (1767–1830), the renowned French statesman and writer.]

5. "J. D. Michaelis in Göttingen [Johann Daniel Michaelis (1717–91), professor of theology in the University of Göttingen] had propounded this unusual opinion even before Kant. But the author of this article [viz., Constant] has informed me that Kant is the philosopher referred to[6] in this passage."—K. F. Cramer. [Karl Friedrich Cramer (1752–1807), the editor of the periodical *Frankreich*, was formerly professor of Greek, oriental languages, and homiletics at Kiel until his dismissal in 1794 because of his open sympathy for the French Revolution, after which dismissal he became a book dealer in Paris.]

6. I hereby admit that this was actually said by me somewhere,[7] though I cannot now recollect the place.—I. Kant.

7. [Kant does say something similar in the "Casuistical Questions" appended to the article on "Lying" contained in the *Metaphysical Principles of the Doctrine of Virtue* (Part II of the *Metaphysics of Morals*). See the Royal Prussian Academy edition, Vol. VI, p. 431.]

no rights, there are no duties. To tell the truth is thus a duty, but is a duty only with regard to one who has a right to the truth. But no one has a right to a truth that harms others.''

The πρῶτον ψεῦδος[8] here lies in the statement, "To tell the truth is a duty, but is a duty only with regard to one who has a right to the truth."

426   Firstly it must be noted that the expression "to have a right to truth" is meaningless. One must say, rather, that man has a right to his own truthfulness (*ver- acitas*), i.e., to subjective truth in his own person. For to have objectively a right to truth would be the same as to say that it is a matter of one's will (as in cases of *mine* and *thine* generally) whether a given statement is to be true or false; this would produce an unusual logic.

Now, the first question is whether a man (in cases where he cannot avoid answering Yea or Nay) has the warrant (right) to be untruthful. The second question is whether he is not actually bound to be untruthful in a certain statement which he is unjustly compelled to make in order to prevent a threatening misdeed against himself or someone else.

Truthfulness in statements that cannot be avoided is the formal duty of man to everyone,[9] however great the disadvantage that may arise therefrom for him or for any other. And even though by telling an untruth I do no wrong to him who unjustly compels me to make a statement, yet by this falsification, which as such can be called a lie (though not in a juridical sense), I do wrong to duty in general in a most essential point. That is, as far as in me lies I bring it about that statements (declarations) in general find no credence, and hence also that all rights based on contracts[13] become void and lose their force, and this is a wrong done to mankind in general.

Hence a lie defined merely as an intentionally untruthful declaration to another man does not require the additional condition that it must do harm to another, as jurists require in their definition (*mendacium est falsiloquium in praeiudicium alterius*).[14] For a lie always harms another; if not some other

8. [the first fallacy.]

9. I do not want to sharpen this principle to the point of saying "Untruthfulness is a violation of one's duty to himself." For this principle belongs to ethics,[10] but here the concern is with a duty of right [*Rechtspflicht*].[11] The *Doctrine of Virtue* [*Tugendlehre*] sees in this transgression only worthlessness, the reproach of which the liar draws upon himself.[12]

10. [As contained in the *Metaphysical Principles of the Doctrine of Virtue* [*Tugendlehre*], which is Part II of the *Metaphysics of Morals*.]

11. [Duties of right are treated in the *Metaphysical Principles of the Doctrine of Right* [*Rechtslehre*], which is Part I of the *Metaphysics of Morals*.]

12. [See the *Doctrine of Virtue*, Ak. VI, 429–31.]

13. [See the opus cited above in note 11, Ak. VI, 271–75.]

14. [a lie is a falsehood that harms another.]

human being, then it nevertheless does harm to humanity in general, inasmuch as it vitiates the very source of right [*Rechtsquelle*].

However, this well-intentioned lie can become punishable in accordance with civil law because of an accident (*casus*); and that which avoids liability to punishment only by accident can also be condemned as wrong even by external 427 laws. For example, [15] if by telling a lie you have in fact hindered someone who was even now planning a murder, then you are legally responsible for all the consequences that might result therefrom. But if you have adhered strictly to the truth, then public justice cannot lay a hand on you, whatever the unforeseen consequence might be. It is indeed possible that after you have honestly answered Yes to the murderer's question as to whether the intended victim is in the house, the latter went out unobserved and thus eluded the murderer, so that the deed would not have come about. However, if you told a lie and said that the intended victim was not in the house, and he has actually (though unbeknownst to you) gone out, with the result that by so doing he has been met by the murderer and thus the deed has been perpetrated, then in this case you may be justly accused as having caused his death. For if you had told the truth as best you knew it, then the murderer might perhaps have been caught by neighbors who came running while he was searching the house for his intended victim, and thus the deed might have been prevented. Therefore, whoever tells a lie, regardless of how good his intentions may be, must answer for the consequences resulting therefrom even before a civil tribunal and must pay the penalty for them, regardless of how unforeseen those consequences may be. This is because truthfulness is a duty that must be regarded as the basis of all duties founded on contract, and the laws of such duties would be rendered uncertain and useless if even the slightest exception to them were admitted.

To be truthful (honest) in all declarations is, therefore, a sacred and unconditionally commanding law of reason that admits of no expediency whatsoever.

Monsieur Constant remarks thoughtfully and correctly with regard to the decrying of such principles that are so strict as to be alleged to lose themselves in impracticable ideas and that are therefore to be rejected. He says on page 123 [of the German translation of Constant's piece that appeared in the periodical *Frankreich*], "In every case where a principle that has been proved to be true appears to be inapplicable, the reason for this inapplicability lies in the fact that we do not know the middle principle that contains the means of its application." He adduces (p. 121) the doctrine of equality as being the first link of the social chain when he says (p. 122): "No man can be bound by any laws other than these to whose formation he has contributed. In a very limited society this principle can be applied directly and requires no middle principle in order to become 428 a common principle. But in a very numerous society there must be added a new principle to the one that has been stated. The middle principle is this: individuals can contribute to the formation of laws either in their own person or through their representatives. Whoever wanted to apply the former principle to a numerous society without also using the middle principle would unfailingly bring

15. [This ensuing instance is similar to the one cited in note 7 above.]

about the destruction of such a society. But this circumstance, which would show only the ignorance or the incompetence of the legislator, would prove nothing against the principle.'' He concludes (p. 125) thus: ''A principle acknowledged as true must hence never be abandoned, however obviously there seems to be danger involved in it.'' (And yet the good man himself abandoned the unconditional principle of truthfulness on account of the danger which that principle posed for society, inasmuch as he could not find any middle principle that could serve to prevent this danger; and indeed there is no such principle to do the mediating here.)

If the names of the persons as they have here been introduced be retained, then the ''French philosopher'' confuses the action whereby someone does harm (*nocet*) to another by telling the truth when its avowal cannot be avoided with the action whereby someone does wrong to (*laedit*) another. It was merely an accident (*casus*) that the truth of the statement did harm [but not wrong] to the occupant of the house, but it was not a free act (in the juridical sense). For from a right to demand that another should lie for the sake of one's own advantage there would follow a claim that conflicts with all lawfulness. For every man has not only a right but even the strictest duty to be truthful in statements that are unavoidable, whether this truthfulness does harm [but not wrong] to himself or to others. Therefore he does not himself by this [truthfulness] actually harm [*nocet*] the one who suffers because of it; rather, this harm is caused by accident [*casus*]. For he is not at all free to choose in such a case, inasmuch as truthfulness (if he must speak [i.e., must answer Yea or Nay]) is an unconditional duty. The ''German philosopher'' will, therefore, not take as his principle the proposition (p. 124), ''To tell the truth is a duty, but is a duty only with regard to the man who has a right to the truth.'' He will not do so, first, because of the confused formulation of the proposition, inasmuch as truth is not a possession the right to which can be granted to one person but refused to another. But, secondly, he will not do so mainly because the duty of truthfulness (which is the only thing under consideration here) makes no distinction between persons to whom one has this duty and to whom one can be excused from this duty; it is, rather, an unconditional duty which holds in all circumstances.

Now, in order to go from a metaphysics of right (which abstracts from all empirical determinations) to a principle of politics (which applies these [metaphysical] concepts [of right] to instances provided by experience) and by means of this principle to gain the solution of a problem of politics in accordance with the universal principle of right, the philosopher will provide the following. First, he will present an axiom, i.e., an apodeictically certain proposition that arises directly from the definition of external right (the harmony of the freedom of each with the freedom of all others according to a universal law).[16] Second, he will provide a postulate of external public law (the will of all united according to the principle of equality, without which no freedom would exist for any-

16. [See the opus cited in note 11, Ak. VI, 230–31.]

one). [17] Third, there is the problem of how to make arrangements so that in a society, however large, harmony can be maintained in accordance with principles of freedom and equality (namely, by means of a representative system). [18] And this will then be a principle of politics; and establishing and arranging such a political system will involve decrees that are drawn from experiential knowledge regarding men; and such decrees will have in view only the mechanism for the administration of justice and how such mechanism is to be suitably arranged. Right must never be adapted to politics; rather, politics must always be adapted to right.

The author says, "A principle acknowledged as true (I add, acknowledged as an a priori principle, and therefore apodeictic) must never be forsaken, however apparently danger is involved in it." But here one must understand the danger not as that of (accidentally) doing harm [*schaden*] but in general as the danger of doing wrong [*unrecht*]. [19] And such wrongdoing would occur if I made the duty of truthfulness, which is wholly unconditional and which constitutes the supreme juridical condition in assertions, into a conditional duty subordinate to other considerations. And although by telling a certain lie I in fact do not wrong anyone, I nevertheless violate the principle of right in regard to all unavoidably necessary statements generally (i.e., the principle of right is thereby wronged formally, though not materially). This is much worse than committing an injustice against some individual person, inasmuch as such a deed does not always presuppose that there is in the subject a principle for such an act.

The man who is asked whether or not he intends to speak truthfully in the statement that he is now to make and who does not receive the very question with indignation as regards the suspicion thereby expressed that he might be a liar, but who instead asks permission to think first about possible exceptions— that man is already a liar (*in potentia*). [20] This is because he shows that he does not acknowledge truthfulness as in itself a duty but reserves for himself exceptions from a rule which by its very nature does not admit of any exceptions, inasmuch as to admit of such would be self-contradictory.   430

All practical principles of right must contain rigorous truth; and the principles that are here called middle principles can contain only the closer determination of the application of these latter principles (according to rules of politics) to cases that happen to occur, but such middle principles can never contain exceptions to the aforementioned principles of right. This is because such exceptions would destroy the universality on account of which alone they bear the name of principles.

17. [See op. cit. in note 11, Ak. VI, 311.]

18. [See op. cit. in note 11, Ak. VI, 313–15.]

19. [See above at Ak. p. 428, where Kant distinguishes *nocet* from *laedit*.]

20. [in accordance with possibility.]

GERMAN-ENGLISH LIST OF TERMS

A

Achtung	respect
Affektionspreis	affective price
Allgemeinheit	universality
analytisch-praktische Sätze	analytic practical propositions
Angenehme, das	pleasant, the
Anschauung, sinnliche	intuition, sensuous
Anthropologie, praktische	anthropology, practical
Arbeitsteilung	division of labor
Autonomie des Willens	autonomy of the will

B

Bedürfnisse	needs
Beispiel	example
Beurteilungsvermögen	judgment, power of
Bewegungsgrund	motive

C

Charakter	character

D

Denken	thinking
Dialektik	dialectic
Ding an sich	thing in itself

E

Einheit	unity
Empfindung	sensation
Erfahrung	experience
Erklärung	explanation
Erscheinung	appearance
Ethik	ethics

F

Form	form
Formel	formula
Freiheit	freedom

G

Gefühl	feeling
Geschmack	taste
Gesetz	law
Gesetzgebung	legislation
Gesetzmässigkeit	conformity to law
Glaube	belief
Glückseligkeit	happiness
Gott	God
Grundlegung	grounding
Grundsatz	principle
Gut	good

H

Handlung	action
Heilige, der	Holy One
Heteronomie	heteronomy
Hyperphysik	hyperphysics

I

Ich, das	ego
Ideal	ideal
Idee	idea
Imperativ	imperative
Instinkt	instinct
Intelligenz	intelligence
intelligible Welt	intelligible world
Interesse	interest

K

Kanon	canon
Kategorien	categories
Kausalität	causality
Kritik der Vernunft	critique of reason

L

Liebe	love

Logik	logic	Regel	rule
Lüge	lying	Reich der Zwecke	kingdom of ends

M

S

Marktpreis	market price
Materie	matter
Mathematik	mathematics
Maxime	maxim
Menschenvernunft	human reason
Menschenverstand	human understanding
Menschheit	humanity
Metaphysik	metaphysics
Metaphysik der Sitten	metaphysics of morals
Misologie	misology
Mittel und Zweck	means and end
Moral	morals
Moralität	morality

Selbst	self
Selbstliebe	self-love
Selbstmord	suicide
Selbsttätigkeit	spontaneity
Sinn	sense
Sinnenwelt	world of sense
Sinnlichkeit	sensibility
Sitten	morals
sittliches Gesetz	moral law
Sittlichkeit	morality
Sollen	ought
Spiel	play
Standpunkt	standpoint
synthetisch-praktische Sätze	synthetic practical propositions

N

Natur	nature
Naturnotwendig-keit	natural necessity
Neigung	inclination
Nötigung	necessitation
Notwendigkeit	necessity

O

Ordnung	order

P

Person	person
Pflicht	duty
Philosophie	philosophy
Physik	physics
Popularität	popularity
pragmatisch	pragmatic
Preis	price
Prinzip	principle
Propädeutik	propaedeutic
Psychologie	psychology

T

Tätigkeit	activity
Teilnehmung	sympathy
Teleologie	teleology
Temperament	temperament
Totalität	totality
Transcendental-philosophie	transcendental philosophy
transcendente Begriffe	transcendent concepts
Triebfeder	incentive
Tugend	virtue

U

Unbedingte, das	unconditioned, the
Unbegreiflichkeit	inconceivability
Unschuld	innocence
Unterweisung	instruction
Urteilskraft	judgment, faculty of

Q

Qualitäten	qualities

R

Ratschläge der Klugheit	counsels of prudence

V

Verbindlichkeit	obligation
Vernunft	reason
Vernunfterkenntnis	rational knowledge
Vernunftgebrauch	use of reason

Verstand	understanding	Wesen,	being, rational
Vielheit	plurality	vernünftiges	
Vollkommenheit	perfection	Wille	will
		Würde	dignity

W

Weisheit	wisdom
Weltweisheit	philosophy
Wert	value, worth

Z

Zweck	end

INDEX

(Roman numerals refer to the Introduction; Arabic ones refer to the page numbers of the Akademie edition, which appear as marginal numbers in the present translation.)

Action *(Handlung)*, morally good, ix, 390; permitted and forbidden, 439

Activity *(Tätigkeit)*, pure, of the self, 451–452

Affective price *(Affektionspreis)*, 435

Analytic practical propositions *(analytisch-praktische Sätze)*, 417–418, 419, 420 n, 445

Ancients, the, 387, 394

Anthropology, practical *(Anthropologie, praktische)*, as the empirical part of ethics in contrast to the metaphysics of morals, v, xi, 388, 389, 410, 412

Appearance *(Erscheinung)*, 451, 453, 457, 459, 461

Autonomy of the will *(Autonomie des Willens)*, is the ground for human dignity, 436, 439–440; is the supreme principle of morality, vi, vii, viii, x, 440, 444–445, 449–450; is explained by the concept of freedom, 446–448, 450, 452–453, *see also* 454, 461

Being, rational *(Wesen, vernünftiges)*, in contrast to the particular nature of human beings, x–xi, 389, 408, 410, 410 n, 412, 413, 414, 421 n, 425, 426–427, 428–429, 442, 447–448; is an end in itself, 428–430, 436

Belief *(Glaube)*, rational, 462

Canon *(Kanon)*, of moral estimation of actions, 424

Categorical imperative, *see* Imperative

Categories *(Kategorien)*, related to ethics, 436

Causality *(Kausalität)*, practical, 417, 446, 448, 449, 452–453, 457–458,

461; in contrast to external, 457, 459–460

Character *(Charakter)*, ix, 393, 398–399

Conformity to law *(Gesetzmässigkeit)*, universal conformity of actions in general, 402–403

Counsels of prudence *(Ratschläge der Klugheit)*, 416–417, 418–419

Critique of reason *(Kritik der Vernunft)*, of pure practical and of pure speculative, v, ix, x, 391, 405, 445

Dialectic *(Dialektik)*, natural, of practical reason, 405, 455–456

Dignity *(Würde)*, as the inner, unconditional worth of the moral law, 411, 425, 436–437; of a rational being, 434–435, 437–438, 439, 440

Division of labor *(Arbeitsteilung)*, in industry and in philosophy, 388–389

Duty *(Pflicht)*, ix, 400, 403, 425, 434, 439; is no concept of experience, ix, 406–408; is no chimerical concept, 402; common idea of, 389; its influence, 410–411; its origin, 412; its pure representation, 410; *from* duty in contrast to *in accordance with* duty, viii, 390, 397–399, 406–407, 421–423, 439–440; specific kinds of, xi–xii

Ego *(das Ich)*, in itself, 451; two-fold aspect of, 457

End *(Zweck)*, 427; subjective and objective, 427–429, 430–431; material or relative, 427–428, 436; end in itself, vii, viii, 428–430; order of ends, 450; subject of all ends, 431,

73

437–438; kingdom of ends, *see* Kingdom

Ethics (*Ethik*), 387–388

Example (*Beispiel*), value (or lack thereof) for morality, 408–409, 419, 454, 459; persons as examples of the law, 401 n

Experience (*Erfahrung*), 389, 391, 406–408, 418, 426, 431, 442, 444, 448, 455, 459, 460

Explanation (*Erklärung*), 459–460, 461–462

Feeling (*Gefühl*), 435, 442, 451; of pleasure and displeasure, 427, 460; moral and physical, 442, 460, 460 n

Form (*Form*), of action, 416; of maxims, 436; of pure practical reason, 461; of understanding and reason, 387, 454; of universality, 431, 436, 458; of the will, 436, 444

Formula (*Formel*), of the categorical imperative, vi–viii, 421, 426, 429, 434, 436–438, 447

Freedom (*Freiheit*), 435; its concept explains autonomy of the will, 446–447, 450, 452–453, 458–459, 461; is not a concept of experience, x, 455; is only an idea, 455, 459; positive and negative concept of, 446–447, 452–453, 454–455, 457–458; freedom and natural necessity, 456–458, 461–462; its possibility is not to be comprehended, x, 456, 459, 461; is not to be reasoned away, 456; its deduction is difficult, 447; is a law of the intelligible world, 454; is a property of all rational beings, 447–448; theoretical and practical, x, 448 n

God (*Gott*), as the highest good, x, 408–409; his will as the basis of a heteronomous ethics, viii, 443; his will as supreme cause of the world, 463; as sovereign in a kingdom of ends, 433; and in a kingdom of nature, 439

Good (*Gut*), the, as practically necessary, 412; in distinction to the pleasant, 413; cannot conflict with itself,

437; archetype of, 408–409; conditioned and unconditioned, 414; its objective laws, 413–414; the supreme good, 396, 401, 409

Grounding (*Grundlegung*), for the Metaphysics of Morals, v, 391–392

Happiness (*Glückseligkeit*), vi, 393, 395–396, 399, 405, 410, 415, 417–418, 430; is an indeterminate concept, 418–419; is an ideal of the imagination, 418; as the principle of morality, 442, 450, 453; of others, 401, 441, 442 n; of ourselves, 399, 442

Heteronomy (*Heteronomie*), of the will, vi, ix, x, 433, 460; source of all spurious principles of morality, 441–445; heteronomy of efficient causes (in the world of sense), 446, 452, 453, 458

Holy One (*der Heilige*), of the gospel, 408

Humanity (*Menschheit*), idea of as an end in itself, 429–431

Human reason, human understanding (*Menschenvernunft, Menschenverstand*), 391, 394–395, 396, 402, 403–405, 411, 450, 452, 454, 456, 457

Hutcheson, Francis, 442 n

Hyperphysics (*Hyperphysik*), 410

Idea (*Idee*), in contrast to knowledge, 462; of an intelligible world, 462; of freedom, 448; of humanity as an end in itself, 429–431; practical and theoretical, 436 n; common idea of duty, 389; idea of a pure will, 390; of pure practical reason, 389, 460; of reason in general, 412, 452, 455

Ideal (*Ideal*), of imagination, 418; of moral perfection, 408; of the kingdom of ends, 433, 462; of an intelligible world, 462

Imperative (*Imperativ*), definition of, 413–414; divided into hypothetical and categorical, viii, ix, 414–417, 420–421, 425, 428, 431–432, 440–441, 444; into problematic, assertoric, and apodeictic, 415; into technical, pragmatic, and moral, 416–417; taken as a rule of skill, 415, 417, 419; as a counsel of prudence, 416–419; as a law of morality, 416, 419; the categorical imperative, v, vi, 414–415, 416; called also the imperative of morality, 416, 419, 420, 441, 444; called the practical imperative, 429; called the imperative of duty, 421; only the categorical imperative is a law, 420, 428; and it is an unconditional law, 432, 463; how are problematic imperatives possible, 417; how are assertoric ones possible, 417–419; how are categorical ones possible, viii–x, 419–421, 447, 453–455; various formulations of the categorical imperative, *see* Formula of the categorical imperative; various particular ones, xi, xii

Incentive (*Triebfeder*), as the subjective ground of desire, ix, x, 412–413, 427; as material principles of the will, 400; as sensuous principles, 404, 449; feelings and inclinations as such sensuous principles, 411, 439–440, 442

Inclination (*Neigung*), 413 n; in contrast to duty, 397–399; contrasted with the feeling of respect, 401 n; contrasted with reason, 424; sum of, 394, 399, 405; plurality of, 396, 425–426, 427, 428, 441, 444, 454, 457

Inconceivability (*Unbegreiflichkeit*), of the moral imperative, 463

Innocence (*Unschuld*), 404–405

Instinct (*Instinkt*), 395–396, 459

Instruction (*Unterweisung*), moral, 411 n, 412

Intelligence (*Intelligenz*), a rational being taken as such, 452–454, 457–459, 461; world of intelligences, 462

Intelligible world (*intelligible Welt*), defined as a *mundus intelligibilis*, 451–455, 457–458, *also* 438–439; taken as another standpoint, 458, 461–462

Interest (*Interesse*), defined, 413 n, 460 n; moral and empirical, ix, 449–450, 460 n, 462; moral, 401 n, 461–463; in general, 432, 448–450

Intuition, sensuous (*Anschauung, sinnliche*), 452, 454

Judgment, faculty of (*Urteilskraft*), 393, 407, 448, 450–451

Judgment, power of (*Beurteilungsvermögen*), practical and theoretical, 404, 412; ordinary moral judgment, 412, 436

Kingdom of ends (*Reich der Zwecke*), vi, vii, viii, 433–435; is only an ideal, vi, 433; sovereign of and members of, 434; as a kingdom of nature, 436, 436 n, 438–439

Law (*Gesetz*), concept of, vi, 416, 446; laws of nature and of freedom, 387, 452–454, 463; in contrast to a mere rule, vii, viii, 389, 416; in contrast to a maxim, vi, vii, viii, 400–401, 400 n, 420, 421 n, 427–429

Legislation (*Gesetzgebung*), universal, 403, 431–433, 447, 449

Logic (*Logik*), 387; as pure formal philosophy, 388; general logic as distinct from transcendental philosophy, 390; pure and applied, 410 n

Love (*Liebe*), practical as distinct from that of inclination, 399; duties of, 430 n

Lying (*Lüge*), vii, 402–403; *see also* 429–430, 441

Market price (*Marktpreis*), 434–435

Mathematics (*Mathematik*), 417; pure and applied, 410 n

Matter (*Materie*), of action, 416; of maxims, 436; of the will, 437, 461

Maxim (*Maxime*), is the subjective principle of volition, vi, vii, viii, 400 n, 421 n, 425, 438–439, 449; their form, matter, and complete determination, 435–437

Means and end (*Mittel und Zweck*), defined, vii, 427–428; *compare* 416–418, 428–430

Metaphysics (*Metaphysik*), pure but not merely formal philosophy, 388, 390, 412; division into metaphysics of nature and metaphysics of morals, xi, 387, 388

Metaphysics of Morals (*Metaphysik der Sitten*), 388–390; in contrast to popular moral philosophy, 392, 393–395, 409–410, 426–427; in contrast to a critique of practical reason, 391–392, 445; the foundation of, 391–392; pure and applied, 410 n; the boundaries of, 444; Kant's work by this name published in 1797, v, vi, x, xi, xii, xiii, 391, 421 n

Misology (*Misologie*), 395

Morality (*Moralität*), supreme principle of, vi, viii, 392, 463; what this principle consists of, 434, 435, 439; it follows from autonomy of the will, 453

Morality (*Sittlichkeit*), is not derived from examples, 408, 425–426; must be derived from freedom of the will, 447, 448–449, 453–454, 460–461; is valid for all rational beings, 447–448; only it has intrinsic worth, 435; principles thereof holding in other systems, 432–433, 441–443; is no phantom of imagination, 407; is no chimerical idea, 445

Moral law (*sittliches Gesetz*), is the same as practical law, 389–390, 408, 410; is imposed by us upon ourselves, 401 n, 426–427, 437, 449–450, 461

Morals (*Moral*), as the rational part of ethics, 388; the necessity of, 389; pure and applied, 389–391, 411–412; popular, 392; its procedure in bringing an idea of reason closer to feeling, 436, 436 n, 437

Morals (*Sitten*), system of, 391–392 404, 436, 443

Motive (*Bewegungsgrund*), objective ground of volition, 427; moral and

empirical, viii, ix, 389, 390–391, 411, 458, 462

Natural necessity (*Naturnotwendigkeit*), 446; is a heteronomy of efficient causes, 446; is not a concept of experience, 455; compared with freedom, 455–457

Nature (*Natur*), formally as the existence of things, 421; is a concept of understanding, 455; rational nature as an end in itself, 429, 438–439; laws of nature, 421–423, 431, 452–453, 458–459; doctrine of nature (physics), 387, 427; philosophy of nature, xi, 387, 427

Necessitation (*Nötigung*), of the will by the moral law, 413, 425, 434

Necessity (*Notwendigkeit*), absolute, of the moral law, 389, 416–418, 425, 442, 463; subjective and objective, 413, 449; practical, 415

Needs (*Bedürfnisse*), as the cause of inclinations, 413 n, 428, 434

Obligation (*Verbindlichkeit*), moral, its ground, 389, 450; its concept, 391, 439

Order (*Ordnung*), distinction between that of efficient causes and that of ends, 450, 454, 457, 458

Ought (*Sollen*), what ought to happen in contrast to what does happen, 388, 414, 427, 449–450, 454, 455, 460, 463

Perfection (*Vollkommenheit*), moral, the ideal of, 408–409; as spurious principle of morality, 410, 442, 443–444

Person (*Person*), in contrast to nonrational things, vii, 428, 429–430, 438; as an example of the law, 401 n; in contrast to condition, 450; better, 454–455

Philosophy (*Philosophie*), Greek, 387; formal and material, 388, 389–390, 410 n; pure and empirical, 388, 389–390, 410 n; speculative, 411–412, 426–427, 456, 461; of nature, 427; practical, 405, 409, 411–412, 427, 448; precarious position of, 425; extreme limit of, 455–457; striving in its principles to reach the very limit of human reason, 463

Philosophy (*Weltweisheit*), natural and moral, 387; moral, 389; universal practical, 390; popular, 406; pure practical philosophy taken as metaphysics of morals, 410

Physics (*Physik*), 387; rational and empirical, 388

Play (*Spiel*), unpurposive, of our mental powers, 435

Pleasant, the (*Angenehme, das*), in distinction to the good (*see* the Good), 413; *compare also* 401, 413 n, 443 n, 450

Plurality (*Vielheit*), of the objects (ends) of the will, vii, 436

Popularity (*Popularität*), philosophical, 391, 409–410

Pragmatic (*pragmatisch*), 417 n, 419

Price (*Preis*), in contrast to dignity, 434–435; is the same as relative worth, 435; division into affective price and market price, 434–435

Principle (*Grundsatz*), practical, 390; a priori, 425–426

Principle (*Prinzip*), practical as the formal determinant of the will in contrast to material incentives of the will, 390–391, 400, 412–413, 427, 463; is the same as a practical law, 427–428; subjective and objective, 428–429; empirical and rational, 441–442

Propaedeutic (*Propädeutik*), to moral philosophy (Christian Wolff), 390

Psychology (*Psychologie*), in contrast to metaphysics, 390–391

Qualities (*Qualitäten*), occult, 410

Rational knowledge (*Vernunfterkenntnis*), material and formal, 387; ordinary and philosophical, 390, 392, 409, 411–412; its special nature, 463

Reason (*Vernunft*), pure, 388–389; a priori, 408; pure practical, 389, 411–412, 440, 443, 457–458, 461; as practical faculty, 396, 460 n; speculative and practical, 455–457; unity of speculative and practical in a common principle, 391; reason in contrast to understanding, 452

Respect (*Achtung*), feeling of, for the moral law, ix, 400, 401 n, 403, 426, 428, 435, 436, 439, 440

Rule (*Regel*), practical as distinguished from the law, vii, viii, 389, 409, 410 n, 413 n, 421 n; of skill, 416; apodeictic, 444

Self (*Selbst*), proper, as intelligence, 457–458, 461

Self-love (*Selbstliebe*), 401 n, 406–407, 422, 426 n, 432

Sensation (*Empfindung*), 399, 413, 427, 451, 457

Sense (*Sinn*), inner, 451; moral, 442–443, 442 n

Sensibility (*Sinnlichkeit*), 457; in contrast to understanding, 451, 452; as incentive, 444, 449, 454, 457–458, 460

Socrates, 404

Spontaneity (*Selbsttätigkeit*), pure, of reason, 452

Standpoint (*Standpunkt*), two different ones of freedom (world of understanding) and of natural necessity (world of sense), 450, 452, 455, 458

Suicide (*Selbstmord*), 421–422, 429

Sulzer, Johann Georg, 411 n

Sympathy (*Teilnehmung*), as ethical principle, 423, 442 n, 454

Synthetic practical propositions (*synthetisch-praktische Sätze*), 417, 420, 431–432, 440, 447, 454; their possibility, 444–445

Taste (*Geschmack*), 427, 434, 435, 444

Teleology (*Teleologie*), of nature, 436 n

Temperament (*Temperament*), in contrast to character, 393, 398–399

Thing in itself (*Ding an sich*). *See* Appearance

Thinking (*Denken*), in general and pure, 390; in contrast to feeling, 442, 457–458

Totality (*Totalität*), of the will's system of ends, vii, 436

Transcendental philosophy (*Transcendentalphilosophie*), in contrast to logic, 390

Transcendent concepts (*transcendente Begriffe*), 462

Unconditioned, the (*Unbedingte, das*), 463

Understanding (*Verstand*), in relation to sensibility, 452, 453–455; in relation to reason, 452

Unity (*Einheit*), of the form of the will, vii, 437

Universality (*Allgemeinheit*), of the law, vi, vii, viii, 402–403, 421–423; of the maxim, 436, 458, 460; of the principle, 424

Use of reason (*Vernunftgebrauch*), practical, 395; theoretical, 391; speculative and practical, 463

Value (*Wert*), *see* Worth

Virtue (*Tugend*), in her true form, 426, 426 n; *see also* 411 n, 435, 442–443

Will (*Wille*), 412–413, 426–427, 446–447, 458; is the same as practical reason, 412–413, 441, 448–449; free will as one subject to moral laws, ix, 447; the pure will and its possibility, 390, 453–454; the absolutely good will, 393–395, 402, 403, 413–414, 426, 437, 439, 444, 447, 454–455; as the highest good, 396–397; divine (holy) will, 413 n, 414, 439; the divine will is not the genuine principle of morality, vi, 443

Wisdom (*Weisheit*), of nature, 396; wisdom and science, 405

Wolff, Christian, 390

World of sense (*Sinnenwelt*), in contrast to intelligible world, 451, 452–454

Worth (*Wert*), moral, 397–399, 407, 426, 428, 439; absolute, of the good will, 394–395, 400, 436; intrinsic, of a person, 394, 450, 454–455; conditioned, 428